Children at School

The Centre for Curriculum Renewal and Educational Development Overseas

Director: Robert Morris

CREDO was established in 1966 to help developing countries with their own programmes of educational innovation, by making readily available to them the relevant knowledge and experience which now exists in Britain. It is an independent public company, registered as a charity, and is financed jointly by the Nuffield Foundation and the Ministry of Overseas Development. Information about CREDO's activities can be obtained from its offices at Tavistock House South, Tavistock Square, London W.C.1.

Children at School

Primary Education in Britain Today

Published for the
Centre for Curriculum Renewal and Educational
Development Overseas by

HEINEMANN · LONDON

Heinemann Educational Books Ltd

LONDON EDINBURGH MELBOURNE TORONTO
AUCKLAND SINGAPORE JOHANNESBURG
HONG KONG NAIROBI IBADAN

Hardback edition SBN 435 80450 2
Paperback edition SBN 435 80451 0

Published by Heinemann Educational Books Ltd
48 Charles Street, London W1X 8AH
Printed in Great Britain by Morrison & Gibb Ltd
London and Edinburgh

Contents

Edited by Geoffrey Howson

Plates I–XVI appear between pages 86 and 87

Preface

'What is happening in British primary schools?' It is a question which was rarely asked ten years ago because, rightly or wrongly, those outside the schools believed that there was little of interest here—they believed that dedicated people were going about the old job in the old, familiar way. But it is a question which is often asked nowadays: and it deserves an answer.

The reason for the new interest in primary schools is clear: thanks to new thought about the nature of education itself, thanks to a system which allows experiments to be made both at the national and the local level, and thanks to adventurous teachers and inspectors, much has been tried and much ground has been won. Associations of teachers have stimulated the exchange of views among lively members of the profession; curriculum projects have made it possible to devise and test widely the courses which embody the new approach—emphasising enquiry, activity, discovery, communication; and teachers' centres have begun to break down the old isolation of the teacher in his or her classroom, and to introduce people, at the personal level, to exciting new possibilities.

Two years ago the Plowden Report devoted some attention to the new look in British primary classrooms. It has since become plain that here and overseas, there are many who, as teachers or administrators or parents, would like to know more about these curriculum developments. If you want to move beyond drill and rote-learning, what are the problems you face? What are the methods by which a classroom may become creative without also becoming chaotic? How can teachers acquire the mixture of humility and self-assurance which these new courses demand? What do these fine words mean in *my subject*? These, and a hundred more, are the questions.

The book which follows is neither an official report nor a public relations exercise. That would be dull—and unworthy of the promptings which came to CREDO, particularly from overseas, and led to the decision that the Centre should contribute what it could to the questioning and to the debate. Writers with special experience of curriculum development in the primary schools have been given the opportunity to describe work in their particular field of interest as they themselves saw it. Not surprisingly, few of them found that they could write of their subjects in isolation: and, though the articles have subject-headings, the different parts of the primary school curriculum are so closely connected that the authors have burst their bonds—and have been encouraged to do so.

This preface is a warning to the reader, therefore: read the whole book—not a chapter here and a chapter there: and may it provide something of the same stimulus and interest as would a close, personal study of British primary schools.

Brian Young
Chairman of the Board:
The Centre for Curriculum
Renewal and Educational
Development Overseas
(*CREDO*).

Acknowledgements

CREDO wishes to thank the many holders of copyright who have granted us permission to reprint extracts from their works. These include the Nuffield Foundation and their publishers, E. J. Arnold and Sons, W. and R. Chambers, Wm. Collins Sons and Co. Ltd. and John Murray, who allowed us to reprint material from *En Avant*, *Nuffield Junior Science*, *Teacher's Guide 2* and *Shape and Size 2*; Allen Lane, publishers of *Miracles*, edited by Richard Lewis; the Cambridge University Press, publishers of *An Experiment in Education* by Sybil Marshall; Chatto and Windus, publishers of *The Excitement of Writing* edited by Sir Alec Clegg; Methuen & Co. Ltd., publishers of *Talking and Writing* edited by James Britton; the National Association for the Teaching of English, publishers of *Growth Through English* by John Dixon; the Oxford University Press, publishers of *Once Around the Sun* edited by Brian Thompson; and Martin Secker and Warburg, publishers of *Teacher* by Sylvia Ashton Warner.

We are also indebted to the Nuffield Foundation, the Schools Council and other bodies and individuals who have supplied the illustrations to this book.

1. The Character and Aims of British Primary Education

John Blackie

TO UNDERSTAND the character and aims of English primary education as it is today, we must know a little of its history. Until 1833 education was provided entirely by the Church or by private institutions. In that year the first grant of money (£30,000) was made by the State to aid the Church Schools, but it was not until 1870 that the first schools were started which were independent of the Church and set up and maintained mainly by public money. Even these were not free, the parents having to pay a small sum for their children's education. It was not until 1880 that elementary education became universally compulsory, or till 1891 that it became free.

Until very recently it has been generally believed in England that anyone who can afford it ought to pay for his children's education. The primary schools set up by Church and State in the nineteenth century were intended for the children of the poor, and objections were made to their being used by the rich, though generally speaking they were not the kind of schools that were likely to attract those who could afford something better. The buildings were bare and comfortless, the curriculum very limited, the provision of books meagre, the teaching usually inefficient, the length of stay of the children brief, and the standard of hygiene low.

Few people at that time thought it was possible to cure poverty. It was a Christian duty to relieve it, but that there could ever be a society in which there were no poor people was an idea confined to very few, and generally considered absurd and dangerous. The education of the poor should be limited to what they would need *as poor people* and should not give them ideas 'above their station' in life. The great majority of the poor themselves did not want much education for their children. They were only anxious that they should start earning money at the earliest possible moment. It was only gradually that more liberal ideas spread and education came to be thought of as something which everybody ought to have, and which, for everybody, should be as good as it was possible to make it.

The education that was given in all schools in the nineteenth century, including those attended by the children of the rich, was naturally based upon the ideas then current about children. It was believed that they should be strictly disciplined, severely punished when they were noisy, dirty, naughty or lazy, and that they should learn facts and spellings and figures by heart. There were individual teachers and individual schools in which more enlightened practices were followed, but, in general, strictness, insistence upon sitting still and quiet, endless repetition and the learning of facts were thought to be the only way to teach, and the right one. The story of how this system changed to the freedom and informality of today is tremendously interesting, but too long to be told here. Two of the factors which brought it about may, however, be briefly touched upon.

First there was the influence of educational thinkers. There had always been a few visionaries who were ahead of their time. Even as early as 1570 Roger Ascham had published a book called *The Schoolmaster*, which laid emphasis upon the *love* of learning as an important motive in education; Michel Montaigne (1533–92), in an essay on the teaching of children, had laid stress upon the pleasures of education; but such ideas had little influence on general practice. Jean-Jacques Rousseau in his treatise on education, *Emile* (1762), foreshadowed many modern ideas, notably the education of 'the whole man', though he was working intuitively and had only the slightest practical experience of teaching, at which he was not a success. In the nineteenth century Johann Pestalozzi (1746–1827) first began to observe the behaviour of children systematically, and founded a school in which he could put his ideas into practice, while Friedrich Froebel (1782–1852) was the first to realize the importance of play as a means of learning. John Dewey (1859–1952) emphasized the social aspects of education and the importance of problem-solving. In our own times Jean Piaget

(b. 1896) has, through the detailed and systematic observation of children, revealed much about the stages of their learning, some of which the earlier intuitive thinkers had guessed at, and has reinforced much that was already happening in English primary schools and encouraged them to go further.

It is difficult to estimate at all precisely the influence of these thinkers and others like them on English primary education. The complete absence, since 1926, of a centralized curriculum and of what were known in England as Standards (in U.S.A. Grades) and the freedom of the English teacher to frame his own syllabus and follow his own methods, makes such an exercise almost impossible. What is beyond doubt is that it is the principles of Rousseau, Pestalozzi, Froebel, Dewey and Piaget which are most clearly to be found in action in the most advanced primary schools today.

The second factor which brought about the change from formality to informality was the freedom of the teacher, to which I have just referred. This freedom is, so far as I am aware, unparalleled in any other country in the world and it is of such importance that I must deal with it in some detail. In the period 1862–98 it did not exist. Teachers had to follow a curriculum which had been centrally devised. Their pupils were examined once a year by Her Majesty's Inspectors of Schools, and the amount of salary the teachers received depended in part upon the success of their pupils in this examination. This system was known as 'Payment by results' and anything less free and liberal can hardly be imagined. When the system was abolished in 1898 a process began in which less and less was laid down by the central authority and more and more left to the initiative of the teachers. H.M. Inspectors ceased to be examiners, dreaded and often hated by the teachers, and became increasingly advisers and friends. In 1926, as I have said, the old Standards were abolished and it was left to each individual school to decide what was to be studied in each year and on what principles (age or ability) children were to be promoted.

Since 1926 the responsibility for framing the curriculum, for choosing what subjects it is to include, and what books are to be used, for organizing the school and for deciding what methods are to be employed has been totally removed from the central authority and left in the hands of the teachers. The Education Act of 1944 laid down only two conditions—first that parents should see that their children were educated according to their 'age, ability and aptitude' and secondly, that, subject to a conscience clause, all schools receiving public grants should give religious instruction. The first condition means that there is no obligation of school attendance in England. Nearly all children do of course attend school, but, if a parent can satisfy the authorities that his child is being satisfactorily educated at home, he is within the law; that this is no empty right is shown by a recent case in which the Courts upheld a person who claimed that she was doing just this. To the second condition I shall return later.

If the freedom granted to the teachers is wide, the responsibility is heavy. It may be thought too heavy. The fact that nothing like it is to be found in any other country suggests that the arguments in its favour are not overwhelming. In many countries the curriculum, in all its detail, the books to be used and the methods to be employed, are laid down by the central authority and no deviation from them allowed. The job of the Inspector is to see that the intentions of the authority are put into effect. Even in the United States, where there is no central educational authority and where the authority of the individual state is delegated to numerous smaller units called 'School systems', it yet remains true that the curriculum is drawn up by professional educationalists employed for that purpose and not by the teachers who have to use it.

It is obvious that the centrally devised curriculum has some advantages. It ensures detailed guidance for the weakest teachers even if it limits the initiative of the best. It ensures too that the curriculum and all that is connected with it has been drawn up by experts and that all schools have, if not an equal chance, at least the same material on which to work. It can be, and often is, defended on grounds of social justice. It has, however, according to English thinking, a fatal flaw.

The one essential point in the whole educational system is the point of contact between teacher and child. It is to make this contact as fruitful as possible that everything else—

authority, administration, inspection, curriculum exist. If the system fails to work at this point of contact, it fails everywhere. But the contact is a personal one. It is a contact *between persons*, and both the teacher and the pupil must have full scope *as* persons. If the teacher becomes simply a transmitter of other people's ideas and is obliged to follow a scheme of work thought out by somebody else, he ceases to act as a person, because he has not been made, or even allowed, to use his own mind and imagination, to the full extent. The English system does allow him to do this. This means much more than simply allowing him to frame his own syllabus, choose his own books and employ his own methods. It means that he has to work out his own innovations in practice. He is helped in this by his initial training, by the courses he attends after his initial training is finished, by his reading and by the advice and help of colleagues and inspectors, but all has to pass through his own thinking-machine, if the word may be allowed, so that it becomes part of his own personality. Innovation, under such a system, may come more slowly than when it is imposed from above, but it comes more surely because it is initiated by the teacher and based on, and tested by, his own experience.

I would claim further that the English system is much more defensible on grounds of social justice than any other. It allows the teacher to fit all that he does to the needs of the particular children that he is teaching. No centrally devised programme can do this. All children in an age-group must, under such a programme, within narrow limits, follow the same course. This is manifestly unjust, for it makes no allowance for differences in background, ability, choice, taste and state of health. Differences should not be overemphasized, especially those which have a social origin, but to pretend that they do not exist and therefore need not be provided for, is wilful blindness. The English system encourages teacher and child to behave as individuals and each to show initiative and enterprise.

This is a big claim to make and it would be very wrong, in a book written for readers in other countries, to overstate it or to pretend that English primary education is perfect. Perhaps I may claim to know its weaknesses as well as anyone. I do not think that any system is anything like perfect. The ideal of educating an entire population is still a very new one and we all have a great deal still to learn. What I do claim is that a system which allows for the maximum of initiative and imagination at the point of contact between teacher and child will in the end go further than any other.

Go further where? It is time to think about aims. What is English primary education trying to do? It will be obvious at once that the aims of a system which allows so much freedom of choice, can only be stated in very general terms. Such a statement would read something as follows: To allow, and actively encourage, each child to develop his full powers of body and mind (understanding, discrimination, imagination, creation) and to grow up as a balanced individual, able to take his place in society and to live 'in love and charity with all men'. This is very easily said and some would dismiss it as a set of pious hopes and no more. But that is what all educational aims are. It is only when one attempts to realize them that their soundness as well as their feasibility is revealed or disproved. In other words, there must always be a strong element of faith in any statement of educational aims. I hope, in the remainder of this chapter, to show that the aims stated above are genuinely those of many English primary schools and that, however imperfectly, many achieve them.

The first necessity in realizing the aims is to create a physical environment suitable to children. We know, by experience, a lot about this. Children need security. The school building must be safe. It must also not be too large and complicated, for children need security of mind as well as body and little ones can be unhappy and overwhelmed in a vast building. Children need light, air and space, but they also need privacy and small corners and enclosed places. The old kind of school with its row of classrooms, each with rows of desks, and perhaps a hall for assembly and indoor physical exercise, took no heed of the nature of children. The latest English primary schools have no classrooms or desks. They have spaces of varying size, some designed for special purposes, others for general use. There will be a carpeted library for quiet reading and enquiry, one or two studios with tiled floors for painting, modelling, sculpture and craft-work of all kinds, a music room with a variety of musical instruments of a kind which young children can play, places containing mathematical, scientific, historical and geographical material. Out of doors there will be a paved surface for days when the ground is wet, but also plenty of grass, trees to climb, sand to dig in, pools in which to paddle and quiet, sheltered spots in which to sit and talk and daydream. Such buildings, designed in every detail for children and their learning are still exceptional but their number is increasing, because this is the kind of building that a growing number of teachers is demanding.

Children are full of curiosity. They ask endless questions and the equipment of the school provides for this. There are animals, birds and insects to watch and to feed and look after. There are pictures, some chosen simply for their beauty, others to illustrate topics which are being currently studied. But pictures and photographs are not enough. Children love to handle things, little children indeed *must* handle them in order to find out what they are. In addition to toys there are all sorts of things to be handled—shells, stones, bark of trees, leaves, nuts, grasses, feathers, seaweed, textiles—anything that the teachers or children find and bring to school to show the others. Much of England is now urban, and children who live and are brought up in towns know very little about many things which are common and familiar in the countryside, and become very excited when they can see and touch them. When they ask questions they are seldom told the answers. Some boys who asked their Headmaster why bees made their honey-combs in hexagons, received the reply: 'Go and find out for yourselves'. It is no good giving such a reply unless the school is well equipped with the books and apparatus required to find out the answers and unless the children have been trained from the outset in habits of independence. These boys *did* find the answer and it may be agreed that they were fortunate in their teacher as well as in their school, for it is not only a good physical environment that children need but also a good human one.

The human environment is created by the Headteacher and staff, by the example they set and their attitude to the children. This has very little to do with their skill as teachers in the narrow sense. It has to do partly with their knowledge of how children grow and learn, partly with their powers of sympathy and understanding, partly with their temperament and above all with their integrity. A school in which the human relations are good is easily recognizable. The children are friendly and relaxed, obviously happy and confident, kind to each other, usually surprisingly quiet and apparently subjected to no discipline and certainly to no unnecessary rules. It all looks very easy. In fact, of course, it requires endless thought and hard work from the teachers. Yet teachers in such schools seldom look tired or harassed, because the work is so rewarding. The children are not, as they were in the old schools, simply young human beings waiting to be taught or being forced to listen. They are personalities, each with something unique to contribute, each worthy of respect, and learning respect for others and for the differences of others.

It was partly the desire to give children social training suitable to their age which led to an experiment in organization which began in the infant schools (at present 4–8) and which is now beginning to be adopted in the junior schools (8–12). The children, instead of being grouped by age or ability, belong to groups which contain the whole age-range of the school. A child entering the school at, say, 4 years 10 months will join a group which contains 5 and 6 year olds or, in a few cases, 7, 8 and 9 year olds as well. When this organization was first adopted ten or more years ago in a single infant school, many teachers who heard of it thought it utter madness, and of course that is what it would be in a school which used the old formal methods of teaching. With the methods which are now coming into use, to which I shall refer later, and which are discussed in detail in later chapters, it has, however, some obvious advantages. The youngest children find it much easier to settle in when they have not to share their teacher with 30 or more other children of the same age. They receive much help and care from their older companions who themselves learn much from looking after the little ones. It is easier, too, for the teacher when she does not have to cope with a whole group of tiny children, all new acquaintances, who make enormous demands on her time and attention, but has only a small number of these, together with older children whom she has known for two, three, four or five years, with whose capabilities and needs she is familiar, who know her and whom she has trained to work on their own. This organization is known as 'Family Grouping' because it is a large model of a normal family, but it has really existed for many years without anyone thinking it exceptional, in the still numerous though dwindling small village schools with one or two teachers for the whole age-range, in which no other organization was possible. It was the fact that many of these little schools, with their warm, family atmosphere were so good and successful that perhaps first suggested the idea that family grouping might have possibilities in much larger units.

The reader may very likely feel grave doubts about what I have described. He may be ready to concede that under such a system children will be happy and healthy and that the social training may well be effective, but he will say 'What of learning? What of mastering difficulties? What of accuracy? What of the sheer knowledge which is so often needed in life? What of high standards and hard work?' and finally 'What sort of preparation is all this for life in the hard world that follows?' 'Are you not deceiving the children by keeping them in this atmosphere of love and kindness and preparing them for a painful shock when they have to earn their living?'

No system is without its disappointments and failures and no system is proof against misunderstanding or stupidity in those who operate it. The fact that the approach I have indicated makes great demands upon the teacher probably means that, in its most developed form, it is not for everybody, though everybody can learn something from it. There are, however, enough primary schools now in England which conform substantially to the model I have described to make me feel quite confident in making the following assertions.

First, far from the children being inferior either in terms of hard work, accuracy and general achievement, to those taught in a more traditional way, they are markedly superior. They learn from a very early age to act and think for themselves, to use books and to devise experiments in order to find the answers to questions. They perform tasks, not because they are told to, but because their own desires urge them. They are encouraged, indeed they are obliged, to discuss or argue with their teacher, instead of meekly accepting what they are told. They are learning how to learn, not just being taught. When they *are* being taught, more or less perhaps in the old-fashioned way, they know why this particular lesson is being given to them. Very likely they have asked for it themselves. They are, in other words, being educated. And since their education includes all sorts of creative work in art, music, dance and drama and various studies of the world around them, they have a good chance of being educated not only thoroughly but broadly.

One of the marks of an educated man is that he is adaptable. He is accustomed to look objectively at whatever environment he finds himself in and to learn to live in it. The uneducated man is unhappy as soon as he finds himself in strange surroundings. But the educated man is also critical. He does not simply accept what he finds. He may want to alter it. In the last resort he may have to use violence, but he will prefer to proceed by argument and persuasion and will be ready to admit himself mistaken if the argument goes against him and to bow to a majority decision fairly and freely arrived at. It is this kind of man that British primary education aims at producing. He will certainly not fit comfortably into a society ruled by greed, prejudice, hatred and ignorance. In that sense the children in these schools are *not* being prepared for the hard world. They are being prepared for something better by means of experiencing something better in their schools.

There is something else that marks the educated man besides adaptability and a critical mind. He has principles; that is to say he is not convinced that he is automatically right, but has someone or something which he is prepared to admit is a higher authority. England has been a Christian country for over 1,000 years. The number of its people who now, in any sense, practise the Christian faith is not very large, but the Church and the Bible have permeated English life for so long and are so much part of the English scene, that it is still not meaningless to say that England is a Christian country. When the 1944 Education Act laid it down that every school day should begin with an act of corporate worship and that every child should receive religious instruction, unless his parents were conscientiously opposed to it, there was little or no opposition. Even now, when the opposition is stronger and better organized, there is no doubt that the huge majority of English parents want their children to receive religious instruction in school, however little they may give them at home. Such parents, if they were asked what principles they wished their children to follow, would almost certainly reply, 'Christian principles'. If pressed further on what these were, they would probably mention love, kindness, forgiveness, honesty, truthfulness and purity, or, as they might put it, 'leading a decent life'. That none of these virtues, with the possible exception of forgiveness, is exclusively Christian, though all have been consistently upheld by Christianity, would be unknown to them and, if known, would not be thought important. The example of Jesus would be the point on which they would probably insist most. Unlike the Welsh the English are not interested in theology. They are, at heart, pragmatists, that is to say that they believe that if something works it is all right.

The trouble with religious instruction in English primary schools is that it is *not* working. Neither teachers nor children are prepared to accept without question either the literal truth of all the stories in the Bible or many of the dogmas of the faith. The person of Jesus still commands deep devotion, but, generally speaking, religious and moral instruction is a bit shaky and it is incidentally from Christians, not from atheists, that the most searching criticisms of it have come. This, I think, is the weakest part of English primary education at present and the precise place of principles in the education of young children, the basis on which they are to be founded and the form in which they are to be taught and enforced is one of the problems that remain unsolved. Froebel said that all education not founded on religion was unproductive, and the English have given general assent to this view. They would still regard an education which took no account of 'spiritual values' as being incomplete, though the rather vague meaning attached to this term which has hitherto passed muster will not do any longer.

I said just now that the English are pragmatists in religion, that they believe in what worked. This has really always been their approach to education. They have distrusted theories and the experts who thought of them. They were very slow to be influenced by educational thinkers, few of whom were British. Those who were, Rachel and Margaret Macmillan, Susan Isaacs, Nancy Catty and Dorothy Gardner were all practising teachers, and all, it may be observed, women. Rousseau (French), Pestalozzi (Swiss), Froebel (German), Dewey (American), Piaget (Swiss) have perhaps been the most powerful sources of influence, but it was an influence much disguised by being mediated through interpreters. It is probable that few English teachers have actually read any of the books of which these men were the authors. They have put their faith in practical experience; have evolved a system in which practical experience is given the power and have some splendid achievements to record. In future they may have to listen more to the theorist and to the researcher than they have done in the past. Indeed they are already doing this. If they do it with a wary and critical ear they may benefit, but if they ever allow the theorist to take over, they may throw away all that they have gained, and destroy the unique contribution that England has made to primary education, the freedom of the teacher at the point where freedom really matters.

*　　*　　*　　*　　*

The preceding paragraphs of this chapter deal specifically with primary education in England and Wales. All that is said in them does not necessarily apply to Scotland, where education is quite separately administered. For example, the historical development of primary education in Scotland followed different lines. From the start there was a more widespread interest in providing education for all social levels in the community and all the stages of education have been more readily available to a much broader social spectrum. Again, primary education in Scotland has generally been allotted a rather larger share of each child's period of compulsory education. Whereas in England the ten years of compulsory education are divided into six years of primary and four years of secondary, the corresponding figures in Scotland are seven and three. The Scottish age of transfer to secondary education is about $12\frac{1}{2}$ rather than

11½. In religious education in Scotland the Secretary of State and his officers play no part at all.

These differences, however, do not appreciably affect either the basic philosophy or the accepted aims and practices of primary education. These are in general the same in Scotland as in England and Wales. A memorandum, *Primary Education in Scotland*, published in 1965 gives an appraisal of the principles on which it is considered primary education should be based and of the practices which have characterized the best schools over the past decade. The changes in the curriculum and teaching methods, and in class and school organization, and in facilities generally, not only have regard for what is known about the growth and development of children but also ensure that the curricular content and the school environment are relevant to the modern world in which the child lives. The pattern of change and the rate of change may vary considerably, of course, from school to school.

FOR FURTHER READING

Blackie, John, *Inside the Primary School*, H.M.S.O., 1967, 3rd ed., 1968.

Blyth, W. A. L., *English Primary Education*, 2 vols., Routledge & Kegan Paul, 1965.

Central Advisory Council for Education, *Children and their Primary Schools*, 2 vols. (the Plowden Report), H.M.S.O., 1967.

Ministry of Education (now Dept. of Education and Science), *Primary Education*, H.M.S.O., 1959.

Razzell, Arthur, *Juniors*, Penguin, 1968.

Scottish Education Department, *Primary Education in Scotland*, H.M.S.O., 1965.

2. Teaching English as the Mother Tongue

D. D. Mackay

PRIMARY EDUCATION in Great Britain is sometimes described as being the finest in the world. We like to think this about our schools and the education they provide. The justification for such a claim lies in the fact that some primary schools achieve outstanding results with all their children. In these schools teachers have been concerned to develop in all children a wide range of interests. When the time comes for the children to go to secondary schools they do so with enthusiasm and pleasure at the prospects before them. Such children will have learned to behave as responsible members of a community, aware of themselves and sensitive to the needs of others. They will have intellectual achievements related to their own abilities. They will have shared, on many different levels and according to their varying tastes and inclinations, imaginative literature, mathematical experience, art, music, physical education and a number of creative crafts. They will have worked in a carefully prepared environment, will have been encouraged to experiment and to choose from a wide field of available studies, and at every stage will have been encouraged to use their native language.

Our best schools, although relatively few in number, do reach this high standard and these schools may be found throughout Britain. Many more schools, for causes that cannot easily be overcome (social conditions, too frequent changes of staff and, in some urban areas, a mobile child population) are unable to do all they would like. Other schools have aims different from those already mentioned and put their faith in more formal approaches to primary school education; and some are simply indifferent or poor by any standards.

That it is possible to have schools with such varying standards and differing aims is due partly to local conditions and partly to the considerable freedom that headteachers are allowed: our schools vary as much as the people who run them.

The differences between schools in the quality of education, in buildings and equipment, reflect different responses to the educational changes that have been taking place. Forty years ago many classrooms had desks and seats fixed to the floor in rows, each row stepped higher than the one in front, so that the teacher could see every child at a glance. Nothing could be hidden from her. The walls were bare except for official notices (one of which might have read 'Maximum Accommodation—72'). Each teacher had a cane or a leather strap with which to punish children. The classes were silent except for the voice of the teacher and the squeak of slate pencil on slate. Textbooks, exercise books and copy books were stored in locked cupboards. The stout easels bore boards full of work to be done. The children came into the classes, their feet faltering between marching and walking. They took their seats in order of scholastic merit and sat quietly. During registration they learned to spell the words the teacher had already put on the blackboard (believe, receive, remember, beginning, . . .). Each word was copied five times; there would be a test later. Then there were sums to do, but before this the children chanted the multiplication tables. While they did this altogether each child felt confident, and sang the tables clearly. It was only when asked to do it alone that some voices faltered and died away. The board brimmed with sums and the pencils scratched and tapped to the end of the period. The old, brown readers were taken from the cupboard and given out by monitors. Everyone knew the page and the teacher would call the name of the first child to read aloud. Round the class one after another the children read. The good readers did so quickly and with expression; the poorer readers stumbled, were prompted and read without understanding, in embarrassment and pain. After reading, the children learned the names of capes, bays and islands, rivers and mountains, or they heard of battles and of kings and queens. The days passed with the teacher trying to stuff her class with facts to be remembered and recited to order. The facts were often fragmented and unrelated and the children were not required to think independently or creatively. There were far too many children for the teacher to accept as individuals. There were only classified groups of 'good', 'medium good' and 'poor' children. She was limited and defeated by the numbers of children in her class, by lack of space and equipment. She was bound by the necessity to follow the syllabus carefully, as required by the headteacher and the Inspector. Only a few children she taught would succeed through their own abilities in reaching secondary schools and only a tiny percentage would go to university. The rest were destined to become clerks, shop-assistants, domestic servants and labourers.

Cracks were beginning to appear in this sytem before the Second World War. In the upheaval of the war years little could be done to put into practice the ideas that were to reshape our schools so that they would more adequately meet the needs of a changed society. Universal secondary education was established by the 1944 Education Act. The old schools were re-organized and primary schools, as we know them today, were brought into being—but with a rope tied round their necks. The much criticized '11 +' selection examination denied to the junior school the freedom that was afforded the infant school. Recent changes in secondary schools have made it possible for many local education authorities* to abandon the original examination. Today most junior schools and all infant schools are able to educate children in the way they think best. The freedom they enjoy is now very considerable and, where other circumstances are favourable, the children attending them participate in a rich and exciting education.

In 1968 the best classroom is perhaps most accurately described as a work-room. It differs in almost every respect from its pre-war counterpart. The teacher is no longer the all-knowing authoritarian. The children are no longer silent and passive but lively and active, assuming some responsibility for what they do. The room is divided into work areas for different

* The State education system is operated through 'local authorities', i.e. county or county-borough councils responsible for education in their areas. There are 162 authorities in England and Wales, and 35 in Scotland.

activities, each supplied with appropriate materials and equipment. The work of the children is displayed round the room. Their paintings and writings are an essential part of the changing classroom environment. Here one might find:

Thinking

Lorries and cars roam up and down the hill like jet planes taking off on a busy run way. The play ground is half wet and half dry blotches of black show where puddles have soaked into the asphalt.

Everything seems quiet except for the shuffling of feet and chairs.

The pipes are cold.

The weather is cold.

The wind blows cold thoughts into my mind.

Everything is cold.

The pictures on the walls seem to move with the wind.

The trees and flowers nearly quake their heads off in the cool shivering wind

The lamp posts stand towering above us, they seem to bow their heads down to the cars as they come whizzing by.[1]

(boy, age 10)

and

Cows

The cows' colours are black, white and brown, and some are brown and white, so that they look like half-baked bread. Cows have big brown eyes that glare as everybody passes, and round the cows eyes they have white. Cows have got soft pink noses which are wet, and they have also got very thin tails which have got like strands of wool on the ends. Cows have got lovely furry ears, but they are not all fur, they have pink insides. Cows have smooth fur, but where the dirt is it is all lumpy; how they get the dirt on their fur is they roll in the mud.[2]

(girl, age 10)

Books of all kinds are freely available—not the cold, dull textbooks that once stood piled up in cupboards, but colourful ones in which children find help in sorting out their many interests. The rigid timetable has become no more than a framework within which the children work individually or in groups. Interests flow from one activity to another under the joint management of the teacher and the children.

The teacher looks for ways in which to extend the work her children do; she introduces and sponsors new ideas, she encourages new enthusiasms. She is not (as is sometimes supposed) a child-minder keeping a semblance of order while the children follow their own inclinations. She has the difficult task of providing the right environment for learning, and of seeing that the activity of the classroom is purposeful; at times she will direct it herself.

Connie Rosen, a primary school teacher, in an account entitled *All in the Day's Work*, vividly describes what goes on in such a classroom:

> We make some fireworks out of tubes of card and tissue paper and colour them and price them. Jane has trouble with sticking hers. I spread some more glue and say, 'Now hold it and count up to 273'. She says, 'Perhaps 100 will be enough.' We mount the fireworks in the Eastbury Farm firework shop and do lots and lots of sums buying fireworks. They complain that there are no jumping jacks or Roman Candles. They invite the headmaster to buy some fireworks in the shop and let him buy a pound's worth and then complain there are none left. They begin the Bonfire book and write about their pocket money and buying fireworks and then find the poem about the Guy to read aloud.[3]

The children now talk freely to one another. They talk freely to the teacher also and learn to wait their turn. The uneasy stillness of the old classroom has been replaced by activity and the buzz of talk. Everything that is being learned is in the course of being discussed. This is seen as an essential part of the learning process. There will still be times when the class listens to the teacher. But when she has finished speaking or reading to them there will be opportunities for discussion. Listening to the teacher will now take up only a small part of the day; more often children and teacher will take part in a dialogue which is constantly changing in subject matter. Sometimes the teacher will be the centre of a discussion, because the children want her to judge what is true or false, right or wrong; sometimes she is a silent observer whose presence alone helps the group to shape their discussion. While she is there, bossy children learn restraint and the timid are encouraged to talk. At other times, group discussion will be going on in her absence. A child may be at the centre of the group demonstrating some new finding or describing an event that has excited him. Interested onlookers watch and listen, ask questions and add information of their own. Then a group becomes absorbed in recording and clarifying their experience by examining it in talk, in visual terms, in three-dimensional forms and in writing:

> First we get a glass dish and a microscope. Then we got a buttercup and we took the petals off.
> The petals came off very easy. There were five petals. on the head. And the petals were in the shape of a heart.
> Its yellow and its shiney and it has lines on it. The shiney part is the inside of the petal when it is closed... Then we got the head of the buttercup stamens.
> And then we pulled off all the stamens and counted them and I had 52. Then we put one under the miscoscope and it was long and spotty it is also thick and covered at the end. There are two things on it, they are called pollen box and fillament . . .[4]
>
> (pupil, age 12?)

The Bee

> The bee is a merchant.
> He trades among
> flower planets.[5]
>
> (Peter Kelso, age 12)

They will show what they have done to everyone; they will meet praise and criticism and learn to profit from both.

These children are activated by the opportunity they have to study what interests them. The teacher accepts it as a part of her responsibility to see that what they need is available. She trains children in many skills that are needed in order to pursue a line of enquiry and she instructs them carefully in what they cannot discover for themselves. She must introduce them to many new things. She must help them to set high standards for themselves, just as they see that she too applies these standards to her own work. She accepts that it is only just that she should set them a good example.

Some of the children come from homes in which talk and discussion take place between the children and their parents. These children have the opportunity to share interests and opinions with adults as well as with other children. School is for them a continuation and an extension of the process of education that has already begun. These are the fortunate children. They have been able to use their language to discover themselves and other people, and to acquire knowledge of the world around them. They find at school that their language is like that of the teacher and they are ready to accept that the medium of education is language, both spoken and written. The way that language is used in school is one with which they are already familiar But not all our children are like this.

Those less fortunate arrive at school with a language-use different from that of their teachers. They have had less opportunity to share interests and experience with adults. They know little about books. At school they find conventions and customs that are strange to them. Their speech and their attitudes to education have emerged from other social backgrounds. At school they have to acquire new patterns of cultural behaviour, new ways of using spoken language and new ways of thinking. In order to do so they need a great deal of help and this has to be given with delicacy and consideration.

The good teacher accepts all her children without personal preference. She accepts the language the children bring to school and sets to work to enable the children to acquire new language skills. She enables them to work and express themselves in co-operative groups so that they may learn from one another as well as from her. By providing varied activities that relate new extensions of learning to the children's previous experience, she helps them to use the language of education and to add this to their neighbourhood language.

Even when written language is used fluently, the spoken language is still more important. University students spend many hours in discussion not only because they need to discover in talk who they are and what they believe, they need to exchange information and to find out what they have learned and how much they have understood. Children have the same needs at a different level, and, they too, use language as the major instrument in the process of educating themselves.

Some schools have been slow to recognize the value of talk in the classroom. Whilst class numbers remained at over forty it was difficult to make opportunities for talk, as distinct from teacher's question and child's answer. Small children talk about whatever they are doing, to themselves or to those around them, and they turn many of the incidents of their lives into improvised play. In this way they begin to learn about themselves as pupils and, at the same time, they make some sense of what they are learning. As they grow older the talk becomes a dialogue inside their heads, the kind of dialogue to which reading and writing later contribute. This will develop the local and personal character of their talk and also bring it nearer the language of adult speakers and writers. The improvised play which develops out of their day-to-day living widens its interests. In impersonating teachers, parents, brothers and sisters and enacting their doings, children 'try on' a variety of personalities. The outer, realistic furnishings of scenes and characters are left largely to the imagination. A few items of dressing-up, a few stage props, a clear space in the centre of the classroom are all the children need to make their 'theatre'. Short and often violent dramas develop out of real and imaginary incidents. In this way children examine themselves and the people around them. They investigate emotions such as anger, cruelty, pity and kindness and the situations and relationships from which these develop. In spontaneous, improvised drama of this kind, just as in their writing, they will weave together experiences that have come from many different sources—from their own lives in and out of school and from literature.

The school attempts to foster the use of language by calling upon the natural curiosity human beings have about themselves and everything in their environment. In the modern primary school this may well involve subjects ranging from mathematics, physics, engineering and astronomy to poetry, music and linguistics. In the past a teacher was not required to deal with such a range of topics. Nor did she expect her children to reveal their private concerns in the work they did. There was

very little opportunity for life outside the school to find its way
into the pages of children's writing books and what they felt,
they kept to themselves. They would not have written:

> The sun is waving goodbye to you all.
> The moon is coming out said the kitten to himself.
> Today I heard the thrushes sing on my lawn said the kitten
> to himself.
> The thrushes are in the garden and the kitten is
> in the garden.
> The kitten is coming to church said the children.
> The kitten is coming home said the children.
> Goodbye said the children.
> The kitten is coming to bed said the mice.
> The kitten is coming to town said all the kittens.
> The lorry is coming to squash the kitten said the mice.
> The lorry is coming to squash the kitten said the children.
> The kitten is squashed.
> And that is the end of my story about the kitten.[4]
>
> (girl, age 6)

It is important to know something of the circumstances in
which this writing was created. In his book *Growth through
English*, John Dixon tells us:

> One day a girl of six on her way to school saw a kitten killed by
> a lorry. Such an experience is hard to take, whatever way we
> look at it. The girl worked for a long time that day, drawing
> and (with her teacher's help) writing beneath each of the
> drawings.[4]

In some of the writing children produce, they recognize
that life is not all sunshine and happiness. In attempting to
understand all the things that happen to them and around
them, they are doing something that is essential to growing up.
That they now have confidence to do this at school is a powerful way of indicating how things have changed. We, as the
adults around them, are fortunate to have glimpses of the
child's private, inner world shown us so openly.

> It is impossible
> for anyone to enter

our small world.
The adults don't
understand us
they think
we're childish.
No one can get in
our world.
It has a wall twenty feet high
and adults
have only ten feet ladders.[5]

(Ross Falconer, age 11)

Alone

The feeling of being left out—
Not liked by anyone,
Where your throat is dry
And your lips feel like the rough bark of the tree,
Your rough lips stick together
And won't open,
Just like an old door stuck
in the doorway,
Where your eyes, like the walls of a weir
Won't open because
If they do
The walls will burst
And the water will rush out.[5]

(Sue Kitchin, age 11)

I hate
going
up in the sky.
when we die.
I hate the
sky because it
is too high.
I got a growling
last night
because my
sandals. were.
wet[6]

(boy, age ?)

The name *Creative Writing* is sometimes given to writing of this kind. It is the language activity above all others which has been brought to the public notice. In the last few years it has largely replaced the weekly half-hour drudgery of written composition. Sometimes it has even replaced the use of textbooks containing exercises such as:

Fill in the blanks in the following sentences, using either *there* or *their* . . .

Correct the following sentences . . .

Combine each of the following pairs of sentences without the use of a conjunction . . .

Give the meaning of each of the following words . . .

Complete the following similes . . .

In the case of many books of this kind it was a good thing that they were no longer used. But it left the teacher with complete responsibility for explaining where things had gone wrong— for not everyone triumphs all the time. We naturally like to show off the best and the most interesting work our children have done. But it is important that we do not pretend that everything they do is like this. There are many unsuccessful attempts and there are some failures.

Learning where the writing went wrong and learning to accept help and criticism are important ways in which children gain greater control over their writing. With the right kind of encouragement most children will have written a great deal in one term. They will have written prose and poetry in a variety of styles and on many different subjects. They will have written in their own way, so that they 'sound' like children and not like stilted adults. Their teacher is careful not to provide them with a list of do's and don'ts that curb the flow of their writing without influencing its power to communicate thought and feeling. But neither does she leave them to write in ignorance.

She is aware of the need to instruct and inform her children and *also* to let them absorb the influence of talkers and writers of all kinds. She does not overlook the fact that her children encounter difficulties with handwriting, with spelling and punctuation, with grammatical usage, with the meanings of words, with understanding discussions, stories and poems. She may, from time to time, construct an exercise to help them to correct a certain mistake. She knows that there is no book that will help her to do this in exactly the way her children need it. Nor is there a book that will help her to decide about the *quality* of her children's writing. It is her knowledge and her taste that will enable her to assess how well her children are able to use written language and how appropriate this is to its subject and its audience. In all these matters (and more), she must be guided by her own awareness of how the language works and by her own qualities as a reader and writer.

Instead of the reluctant prose that once spluttered from chewed pens there are now poems and other stories in great profusion. Often these have a freshness of vision that adults envy, and an honesty they find hard to emulate. They are, for the most part, written with enthusiasm and they arise without warning from the day's activities. Often they are untidy—being scored with correction and re-writing. Sometimes they are very private and sometimes they are written for everyone to read. This new kind of writing is no longer an exercise passing between teacher and pupil. Now it is more likely to be a public statement of children's involvement with experience and, when finished, it is likely to be written out neatly and 'published' in the classroom or around the school.

If it appears to the visitor that a class 'just writes' then this is because the art of the teacher is hidden from sight. What the children record of their thoughts and feelings is at any one time only a small part of the activities which have given them form and substance. What stories and poems, what sights and sounds, what emotions and how much talk went into their making are never very obvious, except when words and phrases are borrowed by the writer, or a literary form is used as a model.

The following poem is an example of the way in which a boy was influenced by what his teacher brought to his notice. He delights in the use of poetic devices that are borrowed from his Anglo-Saxon forebears and also from poets like Dylan Thomas and Gerald Manley Hopkins.

Sleep and Dreams

Go perfect into peace,
  Peace mighty-majestic and moulded, mounted

> Upon the satin whipped waves of the heavens.
> Roam in orchards of twilit apples, and
> Drawn by a million vermilion stallions,
> Shadow dappled across the fields of legend—
> Go perfect into peace.
>
> Go perfect into peace,
>   Grave and golden,
>   Free of fiery fury,
>   Bathed in the glowing tears of dawn,
>   Night-washed, night-webbed—
> Go perfect into peace.[7]

(Peter Kelso, age 11)

The success of *Creative Writing* depends on the interaction of many influences. I have written of the way in which an experienced teacher enables her children to involve themselves in new experiences of all kinds. Writing of the quality shown in these examples is sometimes the result. What is less easy to show is the continuing growth towards maturity that we hope to find in children's work as they grow up. In this we are not always successful. There are children who write no better at the age of 12 than they did when they were 8 years old. There are some who never learn to write more than a few halting sentences all their lives. For those, the children with whom we are least successful, the failure may be traced back to their introduction to written language. For one reason or another they were never able to use this second language medium adequately. In their pamphlet *Assessing Compositions* the authors write: '. . . if children's linguistic experience is limited . . .their linguistic output is confined to the nearest approximations drawn from what is to hand—i.e., local speech and popular reading. . . . A sense of the demands of the written language seems to come from reading . . .'[8]

I have tried to show how learning to use the mother tongue must begin with the young child sharing the talk of interested adults and how this must also involve him in a wide variety of events and activities that draw him to make new discoveries about himself and the world around him. It is not long before written language must begin to play an important part in this.

If it does not, a growing sense of personal failure will persist throughout his school days. In the end he will reject what the school stands for and will cling to his 'local speech and popular reading'. For such a child creative writing, and equally, creative reading, creative talking and creative listening will be activities from which he is excluded, and which do not exist *in his experience*. While it is important that we describe our finest work in the primary school, it is also necessary for us to remind ourselves that we have not solved all our problems. The worst of these we have only begun to investigate.

Earlier I described the work of the gifted teacher in a school which offers the best conditions of work. Students in training colleges very often have such ideal people and conditions of work described to them. A student may sincerely believe what she has been told in the course of her training. She may believe that education should be child-centred rather than subject-centred; that the relationship between her children and herself should be relaxed, friendly and trusting rather than authoritarian and formal; that learning with understanding requires a wide variety of talk and experiment; and that in place of the child memorizing facts in silence should be the child who *performs* as a mathematician, a painter, a musician and a writer. Yet when she comes face to face with a large class of lively children she may find that she knows all too little about how to work according to her beliefs. It takes very little time for children without guidance to become noisy and careless in all they do. Their boredom will be expressed in aimless behaviour and they appear to be interested in nothing for very long. To an onlooker the gifted and experienced teacher makes her job look easy. Everything in the class appears to happen without much intervention on her part. Yet behind all the activity there is firm direction, careful training and appropriate instruction—freedom within limits. It is the careful choice of the limits that is important, for it is these that give shape and form to the children's work. The teacher does not, for example, abandon *formal* composition in favour of *free* writing—she knows that the latter does not exist. All activities, writing included, must have limitations placed upon them. Only when these have been decided and accepted will the work show both individuality and respect for the medium in which it is communicated.

In the past the teacher was required to teach and test in a way that was laid down for her, supported by a detailed syllabus and approved textbooks. It is no longer possible for a teacher to have all the information needed at her finger tips. When she is asked for help in finding out about rocks, plants, distant countries, space-ships, machines and so on, she must show her children how to use books, illustrations, diagrams and simple apparatus to describe, identify and investigate the objects of their curiosity. In doing so, children are not only adding to their stock of knowledge but above all are *learning how to learn*. This is one of the most important skills for the child to master and in helping him to acquire it the teacher ensures that the child's ability to use his mother tongue is strengthened and extended in the most relevant and exciting way.

BIBLIOGRAPHY

1. Clegg, A. B., *The Excitement of Writing*, Chatto and Windus, 1964.
2. Marshall, Sybil, *An Experiment in Education*, Cambridge University Press, 1963.
3. Britton, James, ed., *Talking and Writing*, Methuen, 1967.
4. Dixon, John, *Growth through English*, National Association for the Teaching of English, Reading: England, 1967.
5. Thompson, Brian, ed., *Once Around the Sun*, Oxford University Press, 1966.
6. Warner, Sylvia Ashton, *Teacher*, Penguin Books, 1966.
7. Lewis, Richard, ed., *Miracles*, Allen Lane, 1967.
8. London Association for the Teaching of English, *Assessing Compositions*, Blackie, 1962.

3. Teaching English to non-English-speaking pupils

June Derrick

IN MANY of the large, industrial towns of Britain there are great numbers of immigrant workers. They have found employment, especially in industry, in public transport and in the hospitals. Sometimes the father of a family has come accompanied by his wife and children; often the father has come alone and then, when he has had time to find a job, to save some money and find a house or flat, he has sent for the rest of his family to come and join him. Many schools in these areas therefore include amongst their pupils large numbers of children of immigrant parents. The majority are children of parents from the West Indies, India, Pakistan, Cyprus and Italy. They have come mostly from poor, rural areas; in some cases they have not had the opportunity to attend school before. The majority of those from India, Pakistan, Cyprus and Italy do not speak English. Some have perhaps learnt to speak a little English, or more probably, to read and write it. Almost without exception they cannot understand the English they hear being spoken all around them at school here. For the younger children especially, their entry into school is a bewildering, often frightening experience.

In the past when educationists have talked or written about primary education in England, they have taken it for granted that the pupils concerned are English-speaking. However poor a background they come from, they start school at about the age of five speaking their mother tongue. They may not do so with any great confidence or clarity, but they have acquired enough language to be able to join in the life of the school from their very first day there; they can respond to the teacher's instructions, listen to stories, join in simple games, make their needs known and, in time, ask questions and talk about their experience in and out of school. As described in the last chapter, a great deal of what goes on in a good, modern primary school is related in one way or another to children's language development. But what happens when the immigrant child arrives at school without a knowledge of English, coming from a home where English is spoken neither by parents nor friends, where there are no books in English, where, above all, ways of doing things and regarding things are very different from those he observes at school? How can this child start to join in even the simplest activity at school when he cannot understand what is required of him? He cannot name or perhaps even identify the things he sees around him in the classroom; he cannot frame the simplest utterances such as 'Good morning', or 'Yes, sir', or 'I want a crayon'; his tongue will not even 'go round' the sounds he hears the other children making. How can the teacher enable this pupil to join in the activities of the class? How can he educate him in and through English?

To a certain extent the teacher's common sense tells him what to do. In the first place, he makes full allowance for the fact that the newly arrived immigrant child ought not to be 'bullied' into trying to say anything at all in a new language to start with; but while he adjusts to his new surroundings, learns his way about the new building, relaxes while he looks at a picture book or handles some simple apparatus, he is already beginning to learn English. The tones the teacher uses to call the register, to tell the class to line up, to reprimand an obstreperous child, to reassure a shy one, gradually become familiar, as also do the individual sounds and clusters of sounds which make up the substance of the language. The process of learning the new language is already under way; the newcomer gains confidence as his ears grow accustomed to more and more of what he hears.

The reception of a non-English-speaking pupil at school can thus be compared with the reception of the indigenous child when he starts school for the first time. The teacher waits for a certain readiness before expecting the child to perform. But when he is ready, how and where does he begin? He will not simply 'pick up' the language and begin to speak it as if by magic. Many teachers in primary schools have three or four such children in a class consisting of native English-speaking children. Others may find they have a much larger proportion of non-English speakers in their class, or, as often happens, may be given an all-immigrant class so that they can devote all their time to teaching them. Whatever the arrangement, there comes a point when some adaptation of normal primary methods is necessary. The immigrant child's curriculum must somehow be organized so that he learns to understand, speak, read and write English with growing skill. As in most things, learning something as highly organized as language needs itself, at least at first, to be organized.

This is where the teachers of immigrant children have been helped by the materials (and some of the methods) so far used in the teaching of English as a second language (ESL). In the last ten years or so, more and more teachers and researchers have become interested in this aspect of language study. Several universities in Britain now offer courses of study in applied linguistics and in language teaching. Many books, course-books for students, guide-books for teachers, have been produced for use either overseas or with adult learners in Britain. The main emphasis in all this work has been on the need for an oral approach to language teaching, on recognizing that the learner can only master the various language skills by learning to perform in them, and that the oral skills must have priority. In other words, language learners must learn to understand speech and to speak themselves before they go far with reading and writing. Many British teachers will confess that when they started to teach non-English-speaking immigrant children, they tried to teach them to read before first making sure that they could speak or that they could understand what the reading books were about. (Apart from language, the cultural content of many of the readers in use in British schools must be extremely confusing to the child newly arrived from overseas; most readers place great emphasis on pets, on games and toys, and on home and family life which may all be very different from the child's own experience.) Naturally enough, pupils taught thus made little real headway, or, too commonly, ended up being able to read but not to understand what they had read.

The modern approach to the teaching of English as a second language not only gives priority to the oral skills, but shows how best to set about teaching them. Learning English means learning to use words in the patterns in which they normally occur in the language. These patterns are often called the *structural patterns* of the language. The teaching of English can all too easily become an exercise in acquiring or selecting vocabulary pure and simple; this is as damaging for the learner who is a native speaker as for the second-language learner. The structural basis of most ESL courses is of help in that it shows teachers how to select and grade the structural patterns of English and how to teach these to their pupils in an interesting way. The pupils can begin to talk about themselves and their new classroom by using a few simple patterns such as *I'm (Amarjit)*, *I'm a (boy)*, *This is my (bag)*, *It's (red)*, *My (money)'s in my (bag)*, etc. These simple patterns can be repeated many times, and other words substituted for the ones in brackets. As the children learn new vocabulary (e.g. new nouns or adjectives) they can practise the same patterns, and then go on to master new ones. In a very short time, they can say quite a lot about themselves and their new environment, and can do so in correctly formed sentences.

Most native speakers of English have never had to think of English in terms of its structural patterns or of the substitutions that can be made at certain points in these patterns. Once shown how to do so, they quickly find ways of giving children the necessary practice in them. Mature language learners are often happy to repeat new structural patterns in a formal drill-like situation; children in primary school cannot be expected to do so. So for a simple session of oral work, a teacher may accustom her pupils to ask and answer questions as a game (perhaps winning or forfeiting points to make it more enjoyable), often with the children arranged in groups or pairs (see Plate II). Guessing games, using objects or picture cards (*Where's the pencil?*, *Is this a bus or a car?* . . .), acting games (*What am I doing?*), ring games in which a message or question is passed on from child to child, afford similar opportunities for repetitive practice. No one can be more inventive than the primary teacher on such occasions; no one loves repetition more than young children provided that it is fun.

Some teachers provide extra opportunities for language practice by recording material on tape. This may consist of stories (perhaps with an amusing and frequently repeated chorus for the children to say), dialogues in which a child can take alternate lines, or exercises for a group to respond to. Children, often with more confidence than their teachers, learn to use tape-recorders and headsets. This extra language practice is often welcome not only to second-language learners, but to dialect-speakers, West Indian children and others.

Of course, there is more to language learning than repetition, however enjoyable and varied it may be. Children have to learn both to ask and answer questions, to make requests, to carry on a conversation, to express interest or curiosity, to give vent to their emotions, to listen to and to tell a story themselves. They have to learn to speak intelligibly, with a pronunciation that is easily understood by anyone they meet. They have to learn to understand a variety of different speakers. Again, the primary teacher with his class shop, his dressing-up box, his use of music and movement, mime and dramatization, can easily turn these and other activities into *directed* language practice. Dialogues in the class shop (see Plate I) can consist of specific practice of newly learnt structural patterns (*How much is this?, How much are those?, Would you like this one or that one?, They're 6d each, etc.*); acting games can introduce a range of emotions (*how* things are said is as important as *what* is said); physical activity in the hall or playground provides opportunities for practising verb patterns and adverbial expressions. The child's sense of pitch and his control of speech rhythm (most essential in acquiring a good pronunciation of English) may be helped as he learns to beat time to music, to sing simple songs, to say nursery rhymes and jingles.

The teacher must not only introduce new structural patterns and provide opportunities to practise them, but he must see, too, that his pupils are stimulated to use their new language freely. The child's pleasure in things he has made in art and craft leads him to talk about them (*I've made a house. Can I make a car now? Now I'm going to paint it blue*). Group projects, especially ones in which children plan and make or discover something together, are a stimulus for conversation (as well as, later, for written work); so too are the making and use of puppets, and the production of radio or television 'programmes'. Visits and excursions are important for the native child but even more so for the immigrant child who, with his family, is new to the district and often lacks opportunities to explore it. For the immigrant child, language learning is a continuous process while he learns about his new environment.

Thus basically there is nothing totally new or unfamiliar in what goes on in (and often outside) the immigrant classroom in the primary school in Britain today. The novelty is only in the way the teacher helps the children to develop their skills in their new language, especially their control of structural patterns, through normal primary school activities. As British teachers think about this aspect of their work, many find themselves understanding the nature of the language more than they did before. This is all to the good, and it is clear that in some schools the indigenous child's performance in English benefits from the teacher's new insight.

FOR FURTHER READING

Billows, F. L., *The Techniques of Language Teaching*, Longmans, 1962.

Burgin, T. and Edson, P., *Spring Grove—the Education of Immigrant Children*, O.U.P., 1967.

Derrick, J., *Teaching English to Immigrants*, Longmans, 1966.

Hawkes, N., *Immigrant Children in British Schools*, Pall Mall Press for Institute of Race Relations, 1966.

Oakley, R. (Ed), *New Backgrounds*, O.U.P., 1968.

SCOPE, *An Introductory Course for Immigrant Children. Stage I*, Books for Schools Ltd for the Schools Council, 1969.

Stoddart, J. and F., *Teaching English to Immigrant Children*, U.L.P., 1968.

4. French

D. Rowlands

THE TEACHING of foreign languages in the primary schools in Britain is a very recent development. French is the foreign language taught in almost every case, with the exception of a few schools which teach German. The rapidity with which the teaching of French in the primary school has developed in the past five years has been quite extraordinary.

In 1960 French was being taught in only a handful of primary schools throughout the country, notably in Blackpool, in Glasgow, and in East Ham. These pioneer teachers were using materials of their own, or materials intended for older pupils which they attempted to modify as they went along. Interest in these activities was, however, growing, and in 1961 the Nuffield Foundation sponsored an experiment in which a very gifted French-speaking teacher took a specially selected group of twenty 10-year-old children, and taught them not only French but also their other subjects through the medium of French. The results were most encouraging; the children learnt to communicate in French in appropriate areas of language with a very good intonation and pronunciation. The next step was to discover whether a non-French-speaking primary school teacher with some training in French could achieve a comparable result with unselected children. Once again the results were impressive and, almost overnight, primary teachers from all over the country wanted to introduce French in their own schools. As was mentioned in earlier chapters, it is a feature of British education that the individual teacher has a great deal of freedom in the way he organizes his teaching and so it was possible for teachers in primary schools to begin to teach French to their pupils, without the prior consent of their local education authority. What took place in 1961–2, then, was a spontaneous and enthusiastic movement, mostly by individual teachers or headteachers, all eager to introduce French in their schools. The only feature that these teachers had in common was their eagerness and enthusiasm, as their qualifications in French varied from university degrees to passes at G.C.E. 'O' level many years previously.

The position was in fact quite serious. French was being introduced into more and more primary schools, by teachers who had had no special training in language teaching and whose knowledge of the language was, to say the least, inadequate.

It was obvious to many observers that this uncontrolled introduction of French could only result in the total discrediting of primary-school foreign-language teaching. Secondary-school language teachers were already critical and frequently hostile, as in very few cases had there been any consultation between the secondary and primary schools in any area. The secondary teachers were already saying that it was all very well for primary teachers to play around with teaching French, but that they, the secondary-school language specialists, would be left to clear up the mess. It was obvious that unless something were done, and done quickly, there was going to be a tremendous mess to clear up, and this could only spell the end of foreign-language teaching in the primary school.

In March 1963, the Ministry of Education, which had been watching the situation with some anxiety, acted. It announced the setting up of a Pilot Scheme which would seek answers to the following questions:

1. Is any substantial gain in mastery of a foreign language achieved by beginning to teach it at 8 instead of at 11?

2. Do other aspects of educational and general intellectual development gain or suffer from the introduction of a foreign language in the primary school?

3. What are the organizational, teaching, and other problems posed by such an experiment?

4. Are there levels of ability below which the teaching of a foreign language is of dubious value?

5. What methods, incentives, and motivations are most effective in fostering learning of a foreign language?

It is some indication of the very great interest that had been aroused at this time that no fewer than 80 local education authorities applied to take part in the Pilot Scheme and offered groups of schools for the experiment. This was far in excess of the numbers that could be accommodated and finally 13 areas were selected, containing 125 schools with approximately 6,000 children in the age group. The areas were selected so as to provide a cross-section of primary school conditions, ranging from one-teacher schools in rural communities to over-crowded schools in deprived urban areas.

Some of the conditions which authorities taking part in the scheme had to satisfy were:

1. There must be continuity in all pilot areas, and arrangements must be made for the children to continue their French in the secondary school to which they would transfer at the age of 11.

2. Training for all the teachers involved was essential, and each authority was asked to provide a local part-time language course to help teachers to refresh their knowledge of French. This was to be followed by attendance at one of a series of three-month courses held in France.

3. The courses in France were to be followed up by ten-day method courses organized and staffed by H.M. Inspectors for schools. The aim of these courses was to demonstrate the range of materials that was now becoming available for the teaching of French to junior pupils, and to discuss the ways in which they might most effectively be used.

Finding suitable materials for use in the teaching of French in the primary school was a problem. Courses specially compiled for juniors were now becoming available, but it was felt that something more was needed. It was to answer this need that the Nuffield Foreign Languages Teaching Materials Project was set up in 1963. The aim was to produce and publish a five-year introductory course which would be suitable for the teaching of French, beginning at age 8 in the primary school and carrying right through into the second year of secondary school. The project set to work in 1963 and produced an experimental draft of teaching materials which were pre-tested in the same year. The materials were revised and the

first draft was prepared for use in pilot schools in September
1964.

The authorities chosen to participate in the Pilot Scheme
had by this time run their part-time training courses for a
year. Most of the teachers concerned had been to France for
three months, and had attended a ten-day methods course.
Everything was now ready and in September 1964, 6,000
children aged 8 began the study of French. They began with
different courses, for each area was allowed to choose the
course it preferred, and the choice was frequently left to
individual teachers. The courses most commonly chosen were
'*Bonjour Line*', '*Bon Voyage*', '*Parlons Français*' and, in
particular, the draft version of the Nuffield Course. By
associating the Nuffield Experimental Course with the Pilot
Scheme it thus proved possible to evaluate its materials with
a fully representative cross-section of children, teachers and
schools. The teachers using the materials were encouraged to
comment on and to criticize them and to make suggestions
for their improvement, and what has finally emerged is, in a
sense, an amalgam of the ideas and suggestions of a large
number of teachers and children.

The education authorities that had asked to take part in the
Pilot Scheme and had not been chosen were invited to become
'Associated Areas'. As such they were asked to fulfil all the
conditions laid down for the pilot areas. They had the same
choice of courses and the only difference was that they were
asked to begin French in their areas a year later, that is to say
in September 1965, on which date a further 400 schools began
the teaching of French at the age of 8.

The immediate effect of the Pilot Scheme and the Associated
Areas Scheme was to impose a much-needed measure of
control on the growth of French teaching in the primary school.
In addition, education authorities had their attention drawn
to the fundamental importance of adequate planning, preparation and supervision, before any scheme for introducing French
was undertaken.

The Pilot Scheme has imposed a pattern on its member
schools that has been closely followed elsewhere, and 8 is now
the normal starting age for French teaching in the primary

school. The exact number of schools in which French is now being taught is not known, but it has been estimated that somewhere between 20 and 25 per cent of pupils at present in the age range 8–11 are learning French. The number of primary schools taking French continues to increase and it is reckoned that, if this rate of increase continues, almost half of the primary schools in England and Wales will include French in their curriculum by the early 1970s.

The questions which the Pilot Scheme was set up to answer are as yet unanswered, for the scheme has still some years to run before the pupils concerned will have spent a sufficient time in the secondary school for their performance to be compared with that of pupils who have begun learning French at the age of 11. In addition, the main evaluation will be carried out with the children who, as 8-year-olds, began to learn French in 1965 and 1966, for by then the teachers, who were most of them new to language teaching in 1964, had had a chance to accustom themselves to both language teaching and to the particular courses they were using.

An interesting finding from tests recently administered to pupils in their final year of French in the primary school was that a surprising number of those who were rated as of 'Low ability' on their performance in general tests, scored relatively high marks in tests of attainment in French. Significantly the tests showed that the majority of these groups of 'high-scoring low-ability' children occurred in schools where tests of teachers' attitudes showed that they were sympathetic to the idea of teaching French to less able children.

Changes in the primary schools have necessitated corresponding changes in teacher training. In 1963 it was possible to study French in only a handful of the Colleges of Education in England and Wales. Since that time over 60 Colleges of Education have established departments of French and in most of these the students are now offered a choice of a three-year main course of French, or a two-year subsidiary course. Similarly, those education authorities which have well-developed programmes of primary school French have also established courses for the in-service training of their primary school teachers in their local Teachers' Centres. The teachers are usually released for one day, or one afternoon per week to attend these sessions which are often organized by specially appointed Language Advisers.

The progress and success of primary-school French teaching would not have been possible without the new audio-visual techniques of language teaching. Most important is the tape-recorder, which is an essential tool of these techniques. Tape-recordings of native speakers enable the child to be constantly presented with a variety of authentic language patterns to imitate, and he is able to model his speech on them, rather than on the frequently less than perfect pronunciation of the teacher. The teacher too has these recordings as a constant pronunciation model for himself and as a guide to correctness of pattern and structure. Tape-recordings mean too that the child is constantly being exposed to a variety of voices other than that of the teacher, and his ability to comprehend the foreign language is being stimulated and extended all the time.

Visuals, which may take the form of cut-outs, posters, flashcards, or of sequences of pictures on filmstrip frames, provide an easily understood meaning for the language which is recorded on tape, and establish it firmly within a visual context. In this way the need to resort to translation is avoided, and children learn to associate vocabulary items with clearly defined objects, and to associate phrases with the context or situation to which they are appropriate.

The courses most frequently used in the primary school are:

Bonjour Line. This is an audio-visual course prepared in France by the Centre de Recherches et d'Etudes pour la diffusion du français. It uses tapes and filmstrips, and there are also pupils' workbooks. Parts I and II normally cover the three years of the primary school from 8 to 11. Each lesson of the course is a story about the activities of French children, which is told in pictures on the filmstrip with the accompanying dialogue recorded on tape.

Bon Voyage. This is a course produced in England by Mary Glasgow & Baker Ltd. It uses seven-inch records and there are sets of illustrated worksheets for the pupils. The pictures on the worksheets are also available as filmstrips with tape-recordings.

En Avant. These materials have been produced by the Nuffield Foreign Languages Teaching Materials Project and will eventually provide a continuous and integrated course throughout the primary school and the secondary school as far as G.C.E. 'O' level, or in the case of less able pupils, as far as the Certificate of Secondary Education examination.

The visual presentation of *En Avant* uses flannelgraph figurines, posters, wall charts and flashcards. Class readers are provided when reading is introduced and there are workbooks for the introduction of writing. All the visuals are accompanied by tape-recordings using a wide variety of child and adult voices.

Parlons Français. This is a course produced in America by the Heath de Rochemont Corporation. It uses 16-mm. colour sound films of which there are 60 for each year. Because of its very high initial cost this course is in use in only a few areas, where the films are held centrally and used on a rota basis by the schools in the area. The Glasgow Education Authority has been using this course in a number of its primary schools which are linked by closed-circuit television, and the Inner London Education Authority is planning to use it in a similar way. Ancillary materials include records and pupils' booklets.

Television Courses. There is no national T.V. primary school French course as such, but both channels have been transmitting weekly programmes for schools which are intended to provide reinforcement and enrichment for pupils learning French. Independent Television has been showing a weekly programme for pupils in their first and second year and B.B.C. T.V. has been showing an adventure story, 'La Chasse au Trésor', intended for third-year pupils.

It is only possible in so short a space to summarize the most important features of language teaching in primary schools in Great Britain. Although these features are shared by all the courses in common use, what is most striking is the extent to which teachers have adapted the principles of language teaching to the needs and abilities of their pupils. The fundamental aim is to teach children to communicate in a foreign language and not (as in so much conventional language teaching) to teach them *about* the language. Therefore grammatical explanations are not used. These can come much later when the child requires a framework in which to set what he has learned.

The vocabulary and structures introduced are carefully selected so that the child learns first to express himself about what is in his immediate environment and what is relevant to his sphere of interest. Gradually he learns not only to describe, but also to express needs and feelings and thoughts in the language. French becomes the language of the classroom during the entire French lesson, and all communication with the teacher is in French. In many classrooms there is a 'French corner' with displays of books and magazines and real objects from France; anything and everything from stamps to cigarette packets.

All learning of new materials is by listening and repeating. Repetition after the tape-recording plays a large part in primary school language learning, and children of this age seem to have a facility for mimicry which decreases, possibly through lack of use and an increase in self-consciousness, as they grow older. But it is not the intention that children should be able to repeat phrases parrotwise. What is being learned must be given meaning and context through activity.

Activity is the keynote of language learning in the primary school. Children are encouraged to use their new language acquisitions in every possible way. In different courses the new structures and vocabulary items are presented initially to the children in various ways, by film or filmstrip pictures, or by cut-outs or flashcards. What is really important is the way in which this new material is subsequently developed and practised. And it is here, I think, that very exciting progress has been made in applying the activity methods of the primary school to the exploitation of the foreign language.

For example, the love of all young children for play-acting is harnessed to language learning. Most courses provide simple dialogues which the children learn and which they are then encouraged to re-enact in the classroom, dressing-up wherever

possible. Subsequently they are encouraged to modify these
dialogues, changing the characters and adding to them from
their gradually increasing store of language. The following is
an example of a typical simple dialogue of this kind, taken
from Stage Ib of the Nuffield *En Avant* course:

CHARLES: Bonjour, Hélène.
HÉLÈNE: Bonjour, Charles. Où vas-tu?
CHARLES: Je vais au café. Tu viens?
HÉLÈNE: Oui, d'accord.
(*They arrive at the café*)
CHARLES: Regarde, il y a une table là-bas.
HÉLÈNE: Oui, très bien.
CHARLES: Garçon, s'il vous plaît.
GARÇON: Voilà, monsieur! . . . . . Qu'est-ce que c'est?
CHARLES: Qu'est-ce que tu désires, Hélène?
HÉLÈNE: Une limonade, s'il te plaît.
CHARLES: Alors, deux limonades, s'il vous plaît.
GARÇON: Bien, monsieur.
(*He goes away and returns with lemonade*)
GARÇON: Voilà, monsieur, deux limonades.
CHARLES: Merci. A ta santé, Hélène!
HÉLÈNE: A ta santé, Charles!

'Shopping' is also an extremely popular activity. Children
set up shops in various parts of the classroom, using real items
from the country where possible, and they buy things from
each other, learning thereby to handle numbers and simple
basic phrases of the language. Plate V shows children shopping in an 'Epicerie' which has been set up in the classroom,
and is a good example of what can be done by an imaginative
teacher with the help of his pupils.

Puppets are another of the common activities of the primary
school which provide an excellent medium for language
activity. The children can first make the puppets and can then
compose their own simple puppet plays using the language
they know. The advantage of puppets over live acting is that
the stories can be extremely simple and at the same time
fantastic and imaginative, and puppets also encourage shy or
reserved children to take part. The Nuffield course provides as
ancillary material a series of simple puppet plays which

practise known vocabulary and structures. These plays are recorded on tape so that they can be used first of all as a form of mime. Plate III shows children watching a puppet play put on by fellow pupils in their own puppet booth.

Games and competitions are also used to provide a lively means of reinforcing language patterns. Teachers make regular use of such favourite games as 'I spy'* and various other guessing and counting games to practise vocabulary and structures. Equally important, the idea associated with 'free-play' or 'role-play' activity, where children act out given situations, has been adapted to foreign language teaching. Obviously the situation chosen must be within the language experience of the pupils, and they should have at their command a framework of language forms appropriate to it. As an example of this type of activity, the following is a suggested 'Imagination Game' taken from Stage II of the Nuffield course.

'Le Pique-nique'

The children are asked to come out in groups of three and to imagine that they are going for a picnic. They first load the picnic basket, saying what they are putting into it. They then set off to the wood, and have their picnic, opening the basket and passing the food and pouring out glasses of lemonade, etc. Finally they collect up the things and set off home.

Exemples de jeu:
    Mets les provisions dans le panier.
    Qu'est-ce qu'il y a dans le panier?
    Il y a des sandwichs, des croissants et des fruits.
    Il y a aussi de la limonade.
    Ouvre le panier.
    Donne-moi la bouteille de limonade, s'il te plaît.
    Où sont les verres?
    Tu veux de la limonade?
    Il est cinq heures.
    Je rentre chez moi.
    Moi aussi.
    Ramasse les verres.
    Mets le pot de confiture dans le panier.

---

* In 'I spy' one child selects an object in the room and discloses its initial letter: 'I spy, with my little eye, something beginning with C'. The other children then try, by means of guessing, to identify the object.

Singing and recitation are of course an important part of any primary school programme, and much enjoyed by children. Most courses allow for the extension of this activity to foreign languages by providing recordings of popular folk songs and children's songs, as well as of skipping and counting-out rhymes which the children can use in the playground. Tape recordings have been a boon for the non-musical teacher who can use them to teach songs to children.

Group learning, where children in a class are divided into groups, with the teacher giving his attention to one group at a time, is a feature of many British primary schools. A great effort has been made to extend the use of this method to the learning of languages. There are considerable difficulties, particularly where a course is entirely oral in its early stages, and does not introduce reading or writing until later. Although the presentation of new material must be made to a full class, teachers have been extremely skilful in finding ways in which material can be exploited subsequently by the children working in small groups. One group, for example, might be practising a dialogue, another doing some drawing or colouring, while yet another is talking about some cut-out pictures. This last activity is shown in Plate IV, where one of the children is putting questions to the other members of her group. The teacher plays an unobtrusive part, only guiding and correcting where necessary.

The children are not just learning a language. The intention is that they should learn about the country and its people. Background information about French life and customs is provided in most of the courses and the teacher is encouraged to introduce this information to the children, supplementing it from his own knowledge of the country.

Where French is well established in the primary school it is usually fully integrated into the school curriculum. Children make puppets, paint murals of French scenes, dress dolls in regional costume, practise French songs and perform them at school concerts, keep scrapbooks, collect French objects of every kind to be used in the shops or in displays. In these and in countless other ways French adds a new dimension.

The primary school teacher is able to bring to language

teaching his own particular philosophy. Most primary teachers subscribe to the ideal that true education is a process of enabling children to discover things for themselves. In the best primary-school French teaching the child discovers, within controlled limits, first that he can understand what is said to him in the foreign language, secondly that he can say things in the foreign language and be understood, and thirdly that he can read the foreign language and understand what he reads. Some less able children will not get very far, but even their modest achievement is still, for their own educational development, a very positive gain, particularly in building up their self-confidence and self-esteem.

At the time of writing, the final evaluation of the Pilot Scheme is still some way off and it is not possible to anticipate its findings. Meanwhile, French teaching in the primary school is likely to increase, and the rate of increase will be determined by the supply of adequately trained teachers.

The next few years are likely to produce also a further rationalization of the age of beginning the language, so that all pupils will begin at the same age, and there will probably also be a reduction in the number of different courses used in the primary school.

One of the most striking features of primary-school French is the extent to which headteachers now regard it as an established part of the curriculum of their school, on a par with any other subject. I asked one headteacher to justify the teaching of French in his school and he replied: 'The children can do it, and they enjoy doing it.'

This may seem a strange justification, but it is indicative of the attitude of those primary school teachers who view all subjects, not in terms of their utilitarian value, but in terms of the opportunities they provide for the self-discovery and self-enhancement of the individual pupil. It is obvious that in this respect foreign language teaching in the primary school has succeeded and is here to stay.

FOR FURTHER READING

Burstall, C., *Report of Work carried out between May 1964 and June 1967 by the French Project*, National Foundation for Educational Research, 1968, Mimeographed.

Cole, L. R., *Teaching French to Juniors*, University of London Press, 1964.

Harding, D. H., *The New Pattern of Language Teaching*, London, Longmans, Green & Co. Ltd., 1967. Chap. 8, pp. 143–87.

Kellermann, M., *Two Experiments on Language Teaching in Primary Schools in Leeds*, Nuffield Foundation, 1964.

Lazaro, C. M., *Report on Foreign Language Teaching in British Primary Schools*, Nuffield Foreign Languages Teaching Materials Project, 1963, Mimeographed.

Rowlands, D., *A Puppet Theatre for Language Teaching* (Including six simple French puppet plays), Nuffield Foreign Languages Teaching Materials Project, 1965.

Stern, H. H., *Foreign Languages in Primary Education*, Unesco Institute for Education, Hamburg, 1964.

The Schools Council, *French in the Primary School*, Working Paper No. 8, H.M.S.O., 1966.

5. Social Studies

J. Backhouse

SOCIAL STUDIES was not at all understood by most of us who began to think about it fifteen years ago. We were trying to improve the teaching of history and geography. Social studies was an attempt to take the best from each of these ways of learning. We had decided that geography ought to start near home and gradually take in places further away. We had also decided that we could consider what happened ten years ago and then move back twenty, and thirty, and forty years through the children's parents' recollection, and then their grandparents'. Perhaps we went to a river and saw that it had come from a source and would enter another, larger river or the sea. We found that villages and towns had been built along its banks. We found out what traffic was on the river, we counted it.

We did not ask why the villages had grown or why they had been built. We wrote down the year when they were built, and said how long they had been there—and some of the work that went on in them. We thought of the river as water flowing from place to place. It flowed downhill, it obeyed physical laws, it joined other waters, and we found out where. We noted its length and made maps and said how fast it flowed, and this work we called social studies. It was an obvious meeting of a little geography and a little history and we hoped that it would make sense and interest the children. It was not a successful piece of work. It was, however, a little better than what we had been doing before.

Now, I think we understand more clearly our aims and purposes. 'Social' has to do with people. Especially it has to do with people in groups and their behaviour together. Everyone lives as an individual and as a member of very many different groups. Social studies has to do with the individual in these different groups. The groups have homes and bases which have grown in definite places and these, and the reasons for their growing, are what we would call their geography and their history.

Children are interested in events that are here and now. The present, particularly if it begins with themselves as its centre, attracts their attention. To extend children's understanding we need to begin with something they already know. It seems sensible, therefore, to begin our study of people with the children themselves. What kind of person are you? . . . Are you patient? . . . Are you in a hurry? . . . What do you like most? . . . What games are the best? . . . Do you like being in a small/large family? . . . Do you enjoy being noisy? . . . What is the best thing you have ever seen? . . . and so on. If this discussion occurs in a friendly atmosphere and the teacher is sincere then children begin to understand themselves a little better. Talking makes thinking easier. The more we talk about something, the more we think about it.

The first group of people which all children know is their own family. We talk about families, altogether, the funny things and the serious things, and perhaps we write about them too:

When I was born there were only two children in our family but now I'm eight there are five children. I like living in a big family, you have more friends.

There are only two children in our family, I like that best. I would not like to live in a Kibbutz because that's really like a big family and you only see your parents for an hour or two a day.

I like living in a large family because there is more excitement especially at bedtime.

Our family is a group of four. The advantage of a small family is there is only a few people to feed and you get more money each. I am the youngest, it's the best. I get the clothes and things that my brothers have had.

There's only eight in our family and so I like small families best. My Grandma lives with us and gives me sugar.

They know their own family, are loved in it and accept it as a home. Now we can begin to look at it in detail. How is it made up? It is made up in lots of ways. There are adults and children. There are males and females. Children think parents can do as they choose and children must do as they are told. We discuss what is father's job in the family? What is mother's part? Should children have pocket money? Should children be able to choose their clothes? Who decides what kind of holiday they have? By talking in this way and by counting we found that only a third of the children in our school had the kind of holiday they would have chosen.

The next unit or group of people children meet is the community of a school. Teaching social studies is almost a complete waste of time unless the school itself is a continuing exercise in social adjustments and attitudes. Our schools should reflect values and attitudes with which we wish the children to come into contact. There are many such attitudes and we should think clearly and carefully about those we wish the children to see and examine and practise. One such attitude is the difficult one which we call 'democracy'. The Speaker of the House of Commons said that 'democracy is taking part'. This 'taking part' should then be a definite planned part of the school's life. Children enjoy discussing how the money that the school has to spend should be used. 'Can we afford more plants or should we buy curtains?', 'Would it be better to buy footballs or tennis rackets?', 'Do you like the colours in your classroom?' and 'Which colours would you prefer if you were choosing?'.

We are a new junior school, opened six years ago, and last year our building was extended. We had a certain amount of money. It was sufficient to build three classrooms and the plans were drawn by an architect. The children had had experience of a new building and many of them had quite clear ideas of what they would like in the newer one. Their ideas included a veranda, a lobby, an extra doorway, an extra sink, a fountain and a swimming pool. So we talked, the architect, the children and I; and the children gained all the features they wished except the last two. We persuaded the builder to dump five hundred tons of soil in a part of the school field. The oldest children (11 years old) were asked 'What shall we do with it?' They replied 'We'll have some humps' (raised adventure mounds on which to play and build). They made plans and drawings and the children talked, and argued and discussed. There came to be three main ideas about what these mounds of earth should be like. The children grouped themselves into sections. The first section wished to have one tall hill. The second section wanted two, smaller, hills. The third group wished to have a longer, lower, more broken up shape. Each group spoke of the advantages of their own plan. The rest of the children asked questions and criticized. Children drew contour maps on the blackboard and side sections of the shapes they wished to make. For three days there was much talk and interest and excitement. The answer was found by all the children voting. John's design (see p. 52) was chosen. The next day we went out and, with John as 'Boss', we built the shape which he had designed, using the five hundred tons of soil. Two weeks later we repeated this process with the design of the new playground. This time Christine's idea was voted the best. She had to make a plan to cover four thousand, two hundred square feet and she chose the design shown on p. 53. Again the architect agreed to build what we wished.

What was happening was that the children were choosing, always choosing. Choice is a very important part of education and to choose well we need a good deal of practice. Much behaviour in and out of our schools that could be called anti-social is a result of children and adults failing to choose for themselves. They have 'gone with the group' without deliberate choice. I do not want a child to do what others do, but always to choose what he as an individual has decided for himself.

Tolerance, charity, curiosity, a critical attitude toward books and what one is told or reads are some other attitudes that I would think healthy ones to encourage. One of the effects of this work is that children begin better to understand themselves and something of their part in a community. Matthew Arnold said that education was knowing about the world and yourself. We know, in our school, that we are all good at something and also that there are things which we find very difficult.

We might be good at working with clay, or making a piece of music, or constructing a bridge with soil and planks and concrete, or using paint, or words, or numbers. All these achievements are equally important and equally praised.

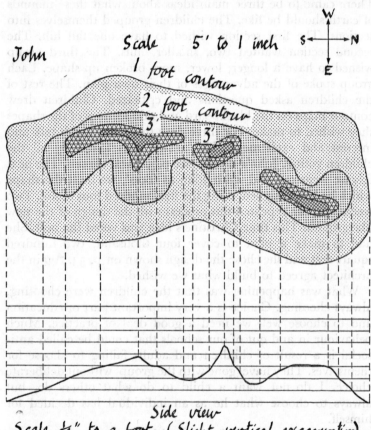

John

Scale 5' to 1 inch

1 foot contour

2 foot contour

3'

3'

Side view

Scale ¼" to a foot (Slight vertical exaggeration)

We try to arrange for groups or classes of children to go with several teachers and live together in a new set of circumstances, for example, at a Youth Hostel. Here each member of the hostel has duties to carry out for the benefit of the others. We sleep in dormitories, choose what we shall do each day, and show others the results. The teachers get to know the children, and they get to know each other in these, different, surroundings. They find out new qualities about each other and so build a more complete understanding of people, and how places and circumstances affect them.

If we go and live in a hotel, a different set of problems and adjustments have to be made. Another set of rules for living

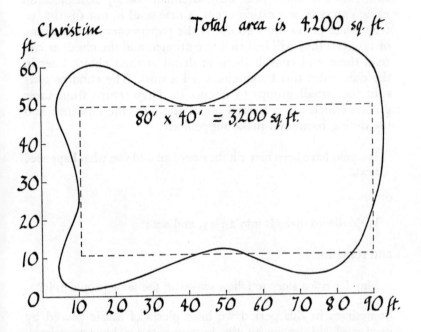

together emerge. We learn from this about ourselves, and about other people.

Assemblies in school, where we meet together to worship as a complete community, provide a good opportunity for us to feel ourselves together as a whole social group.

We have two kinds of assembly. One is the everyday worship which I conduct, and follow up by a 'community lesson'. The second type is the assembly presented weekly by a whole class group to give their idea of a co-operative act of worship. I shall deal with them separately.

The assemblies which I lead are intended to bring together

spiritual and world affairs. After we have had our prayers and hymns I might talk a little about the morning newspapers and magazines which we have every day. I read the papers before assembly and pick out one or more items that may be of interest to some of the children. These items may be about a foreign country in the news, a big advertising campaign (how much does a whole page advertisement cost?), or a piece on using cameras, a sporting event, a new road in our district, or why sweet prices must go up. If the papers contain something of interest, they will be briefly mentioned and the children can read them and consult them in detail at their choice later in the day. After this I sometimes tell a story. The children may split into small groups to discuss it. They return from these groups which are scattered about the hall, the entrance and the dining room and make suggestions:

> It would have been better if the story had told you what happened next.

or

> We'd like to make it into a play, and act it.

and sometimes

> May I write a story to follow on—with the same people in it?

Sometimes in this period we hear pieces of music played by groups of children with the instruments we have in school. Perhaps a group will present a piece of work they have done on 'Which toothpaste is the best' or 'Rocks near school' or 'Things living in the wood'. The rest of us listen with very close attention. Then we may ask questions and agree or disagree with what has been said. We have, for example, counted the numbers of children in families of four, and of five, and of six, and made graphs on the blackboard from the graphs of children sitting in the hall. Occasionally I may ask six of the children whose fathers own cars to talk about them, and their costs and advantages. A short time ago four children talked in this sort of public discussion about how they had learned to swim and the difficulties and how it felt. This was interesting to the rest of us, and again we had questions and talk about it. This is a 'community time' when we join together in our interests, and talk, and discuss, criticize, and argue. It is also a time which causes excitement, and education should be exciting. Often it gives ideas which the children can follow up later in the day.

I feel that for too long when we have had anything to tell we have written it. Now, we more often say it. In so doing, we find children become more able to voice their thoughts and, therefore, more able to think. There is a good deal of discipline in listening to what other children have to say, and waiting to make our own points. These assemblies take place on several days of the week.

The assemblies which the children organize themselves are very different. They may take a parable from the Bible and present it in a modern version and then show the message again in movement without words. Or they will add their own music and their own words. They write prayers and invite the rest of the school to join in saying or listening to them. Sometimes the thought of the assembly will be 'love' or 'care for older people' or 'bravery'. Two things always interest me about these assemblies. First the honesty and sincerity of the children taking part, and secondly the rapt quality of attention which they are given by the rest of the children.

> I am eleven. I am still frightened of the dark. I know it is silly, but this is my fear. Help me Lord to overcome it and everyone else who feels like me, help them too.

This was part of a prayer by an intelligent boy who loved swimming, rugby and other sports and for whom this prayer, in front of three hundred children, must have been difficult to say. Another girl said:

> I have made mistakes, some of them not good ones. I hope to do better in the school. Please God give me help to do it.

I respect this kind of honesty. I think that we all, as teachers, must do.

C.A.S.—5

Much of this work has to do with relationships in school. It is difficult to talk about relationships, one can only give examples. Susan was a little girl who wrote out the menu for our midday meal. When she brought it to me, I would remark 'There are two "b's" in cabbage and an "a" in the middle of potato, Susan'. She would correct it and go to show it to the other classes. Later in the week I went into Susan's classroom to join them during the period when the children chose their own activity. I had chosen to write in white ink on black paper and I carefully wrote in my best handwriting two verses of a poem. The children came to look, in passing, and to say whether they liked it. Susan came. 'Y-e-s, mm— don't you think that writing could be a bit better, Mr Backhouse?' This is right. I felt cheered by the fact that Susan knew that she and I were equal members of our school. It was also a compliment to a teacher when one of her class, who had asked permission from me to do an experiment during the lunch hour, said about her, 'You know she's very reasonable, she always lets us'. One visitor who arrived was weighed, measured, her age estimated and her views asked about searching for Roman coins before she had even got to my office. The visitor was an Inspector. In all of this there is the assumption by the children that ours is a place where everyone matters. Surely it is right for children sometimes to be able to tell and inform and teach their teachers. So when I declare my ignorance of flowers and birds and fish, children can tell me and enjoy telling me, and so the more ordinary classroom situation is turned upside down. Similarly when we, as teachers, admit our mistakes it makes it easier for children to admit theirs, and so to learn from them. By doing this we try to build relationships with the children which are stronger and more real than if we pretended we knew everything and never made mistakes.

It is not possible or correct to make a general syllabus which covers all children, all circumstances and all places. What experiences the children should have, and what development we should plan depends on such factors as:

1. The needs of a particular district, town, school and class— a thoughtful consideration of existing social experience, for example, if, in a district, men consider themselves more

important than women, then this will have an effect which we must take into account.

2. The type of community in which the children live—and its ability to provide different social experiences. How far afield must we go for different experiences?

3. The desirability of planning experiences and investigations in such a way that one piece of work leads naturally toward another.

4. Children should be given time to suggest and carry-through their own investigations and satisfy purely personal questions such as: 'How many people like eggs?', 'Do children who have more money have worse teeth?' (through too much sweet-eating), 'Are small children the fastest runners?'. Perhaps one approach is to begin with children themselves—very directly:

The child him/her self.
Children as they see themselves within the family.
Children in school.
The whole school community.
Other groups outside school.
Examples are:
1. Shoppers—Do they shop locally, or in nearby large cities?
2. Newspapers—Which people take which papers? Why do they choose them?
3. Houses—How did our town come to be built here? Do people like it? How would they change it?
4. A small pottery—the pots are all hand-made—Why is it closing?
5. What buildings are necessary in a town in addition to houses? Why?
6. How does a toll bridge work?
7. A study of two local farms, one is large and one is small.
8. A study of the local airfield.
9. A paper-making factory using water-power.
10. Camping holidays, hotel holidays.
11. The canal and rivers in our town.

This sort of programme has educational aims—all work springs from experiences that the children have had. Children can see organizations which are alike in some ways, and unlike in other ways. They collect data and decide what is important and what is not important. There is a good deal of opportunity for children to choose for themselves.

We bring men and women into school to talk about their jobs. They may explain how they washed clothes fifty years ago, or how they make glass, or drive a cargo boat, or explain about their job as a policeman. They are experts who can often answer the children's questions better than we teachers or books.

Teaching social studies in this way often gives rise to new questions:

(a) Why do more of our children have brown eyes than their parents? (The children answered this themselves after much detailed reading—brown eyes are a dominant colour in heredity.)

(b) Why does wool coming to England from Australia go through five other countries by land first? (The books say that it comes direct from Australia, the captain of a cargo boat at the port says the wool goes through five countries in Europe by land.)

(c) Why do more loaded lorries go South than North on our main North–South motor road?

Children seeking answers may ask the teacher's help—and he may give his opinion—or some fact. What he or she said will be taken as part of the answer; the children come to their own answer. They will explain it and discuss it with other groups of children. They may then change their minds after talking more. They will see that there is no shame in this. To change one's conclusion because of new facts or thoughts is a sign of intelligent thinking—this the children realize.

The children test objects in which they are interested. They test five different types of pencil. They think what are good tests for pencils? Perhaps they decide to test how easily the pencils break, how well they sharpen, how much they cost, how smoothly they write. They test the pencils for these qualities and decide which is the best to buy for school.

Similarly with orange juice, meat pies, different types of glue—and they can report their results to the rest of the school. They will answer questions about what they have done—and perhaps argue about their conclusions. All this shows their interest and the quality of their thinking. It allows the children to see themselves as active, important people.

A group of children of 11 investigated a busy, very noisy, dirty village with a coal mine at its centre. The children wrote:

> The decaying mass of rubble, a deteriorating and industrious filth surrounds the place like fog.
> It is falling to ruins like a child's brick building that was unsafe and wrongly built.

and

> It gave me the feeling of being shut up and confined. I thought everyone did not care at all.

Another child wrote:

> The machines groan and clatter. The only cheery sound was that of a lark.

and another

> Men waiting for their work looked dull and lifeless.

and

> The smoke became spiral stairs out of a whirlpool of gloominess.

On our next visit to the village the children were asked to look for a particular part of its life which interested them. When we returned to school, those interested in the church, the coalmine, the river, the shops, the Roman history, and the history of ninety years ago, formed groups and talked. Then they went to books and with the teacher's help began to investigate their particular interest. Also they talked with people from the village:

A lady in the shop was pleasant and said that there were only three shops and so they all kept their prices alike.

and a girl,

One woman showed us how to make bread like they baked it fifty years ago. We will do some.

We collected objects from the village life of a hundred years ago and displayed them. From these many sources, from looking and talking, interviewing, collecting articles from their families, reading books, and questioning teachers, the children collected much information. All the information each group had found had then to be put together into a complete piece of work. There were paintings, plans, written pieces, tape-recorded interviews, models and statistics. Next, each group held a 'lesson' when it showed and explained all its work. The children had learned from their own special interest, and now also saw and listened to their class-mates and learned from them.

Following these sessions the class came together and talked about the future of the village. They remembered what the village people had mentioned. They had an idea of what £20,000 would buy because they had been involved in seeing £20,000 spent on the new part of our building. We told them that an amount of money was to be spent on the village. How did they consider it should be spent? Their opinion favoured first, some grass in the shape of a park; then either improvements to the church or a village meeting hall built on to the church. Thirdly, they would like the piles of debris still left in the village, taken away. They drew plans for a new village hall. A model was made for the church and an altar cloth was designed and made in tapestry (see Plate VI), a grassy park for children was mapped with a place for older people to sit and watch the children play.

From question-forms which they made themselves and asked the children from the village school to complete, they found an enormous number of statistics such as:

73·9% of the village children were born there;

46·9% of their parents were born in the village.

One boy drew the conclusion: 'That probably proves either more people are coming to live in the village or a lot of people have left'.

26·1% of the children were not born in the village,

the percentage who want to live here when they grow up is

43·5%,

56·5% want to leave,

13% of the people want new shops,

30·4% want a new factory,

8·7% think the place has improved,

91·3% think it has become worse,

and there were many, many more of these. The children made the questions, found the answers, and most important, drew their *own* conclusions. The conclusions might not be my conclusions but they show that the children were thinking, and thinking well. They have also gained an understanding of the way in which a place might grow and why it grows, and perhaps why it, as a village, dies.

We went to another village, one in the country, quiet and not busy. We wanted the children to compare and contrast this with their villages. They wrote:

A serene, quiet village surrounded by animal's voices. A human voice can be heard in the distance. Peaceful fields lay quite empty except for birds and flowers, but all is quiet, nothing disturbs.

and

To me the place was like a present, and the green grass and trees were the wrapper.

or

. . . . . pastures of the peaceful, unharmed land.

One girl wrote:

I felt alone there, as if someone had led me and there in that village I had to stay.

and another child

No black or grey
Of a sad day
Just peace and quiet.

What we hope the children have gained is a knowledge of people living in two different places. We feel that they can see the differences and make sense of them. This piece of work has provided a chance to think, make conclusions and make a future plan. This is what I consider a constructive social study. The children are involved in it, instead of just listening about it. The importance of what they are doing is obvious to them. I feel this is a valuable way of allowing them to find their own success and security as thinking, reasoning people.

When children leave us at 11 years old they have had many socially directed experiences. Recently a class of them wrote out how they would organize and administer an institution. These were the things about which they decided to write:

running a prison,
owning a sweet shop,
having a toll bridge,
planning a hotel,
owning a fish and chip shop,
organizing an orphanage,
administering a camp site,
running a supermarket.

What the children chose to write about showed us something about themselves. The boy who wrote about a prison lived in a home where there were many rules and punishment was strict. Susan wrote about a dress-shop because she is very interested in dresses and clothes. Secondly the children often chose to make a study of the institution they knew best, perhaps as shoppers or campers. The work involved making maps and plans, and employing workers and paying them wages. It sometimes had to show a profit in money. Through doing this exercise the children showed they understood quite well how the systems of our society work, for instance, that shops and hotels have to make a profit and that hospitals and orphanages have money given them by the Government and the Local Council.

The values of teaching social studies in this child-involving way are many. Some of these values can be stated, some become so much a part of a child's personality and development that their measurement is neither possible nor necessary. I would expect this sort of teaching to allow a child to see himself as a private individual and as a public person. He can appreciate himself as someone unique and yet as a member of several groups. I see too an improvement in the quality of his thinking. Our children are interested in the society in which they live and can, I hope, think positively about it and its problems. To be interested in, and challenged by, our environment is to be an active force in our community. I think this way of learning should help the children, and us, to replace prejudices with reason, and dogma with a healthy curiosity.

FOR FURTHER READING

Blackie, J., *Good Enough for the Children*, Faber, 1963.
Sealey, L. G. W. and Gibbon, V., *Communication and Learning in the Primary School*, Blackwell, 1963.

6. Mathematics

Ena Cormack

To HAVE used the word 'mathematics' in connection with the primary school curriculum when I was a child would have evoked great amusement from many teachers. It was a secondary-school word and in the context of the primary school it sounded absurd. There was a subject called arithmetic and it had been considered one of the most important lessons in any primary classroom since the nineteenth century.

The children of the Victorian era learned arithmetical facts and operations in order to equip them for life in the commercial world at that time. There was a need for this. The pens, held in childish hands, laboriously scratched out their sums as beautifully and as accurately as possible. The pages assumed the appearance of an art form as much as an arithmetical exercise.

As time went on, however, the commercial world, while still insisting on a knowledge of arithmetic, added speed as an essential. This meant that the pattern of teaching arithmetic changed gradually from the meticulous practising of 'sums' to an emphasis on 'quick methods'. The teacher found herself teaching a large class of children to perform mental and written calculations as speedily as possible. Many tricks in both speech and technique were employed. Children could be heard chanting in unison such phrases as: 'To multiply by 10 add a nought', 'To divide vulgar fractions, invert the divisor and proceed as in multiplication', etc.

Headteachers introduced tests of arithmetical attainment which were based on giving a child a mark for quick, accurate computation and his chronological age determined the final result. Because a child had lived a certain number of years and months, the assumption was that he should be able to perform certain arithmetical calculations.

If it were the policy of the school that every child had to do a certain arithmetic test at a certain time, then this determined the teacher's method of teaching. She wanted each of her children to succeed in these tests and so their content became the priority in her teaching.

As soon as possible on their entry into school, the infant children began to learn number facts. They repeated these after the teacher and, by parrotting them often enough, they memorized them. A possible plan was to form systematic tables of number facts within 10. For example:

+ *1 table*	then	+ *2 table*
0 + 1 = 1		0 + 2 = 2
1 + 1 = 2		1 + 2 = 3
2 + 1 = 3		2 + 2 = 4
etc.		etc.

Addition facts might be memorized first and then subtraction facts, or the teacher may have had a plan with the ' + 1 table' followed by the ' − 1 table' and so on. Teachers found it essential to have some systematic progression to facilitate the children's memorization.

Every teacher of infants made her teaching as imaginative as possible but even the most imaginative teacher had to admit that her arithmetic was simply drilling number facts and then children practising these. The teacher had to work very hard, since after a year she hoped that her class would know the composition of number to 10—a vain hope in many cases. Her second year's work was to teach her children number composition to 20 usually by building up tables '10 +', '9 +', etc.

These were the demands of many schools for a long time and the children's early introduction to the world of number was this soulless repetition and memorization.

When children could relate number facts to 20, it was assumed that they could perform such calculations as:

$$\text{(i)} \quad \begin{array}{cc} T & U \\ 3 & 4 \\ 1 & 6 \\ +2 & 7 \\ \hline \\ \hline \end{array} \qquad \text{(ii)} \quad \begin{array}{cc} T & U \\ 7 & 4 \\ -3 & 1 \\ \hline \\ \hline \end{array}$$

The chant for example (i) might be: '7 and 6 are 13, 13 and 4 are 17, put the 7 in the answer and carry 1'; or '. . . put 7 in the units' house and 1 in the tens' ', etc.

Teachers coined expressions to help their pupils to reach the correct solutions—and many children did find correct answers.

The next step was to introduce a third column called Hundreds and then 'sums' like the following were practised:

```
  H  T  U            H  T  U
  4  0  6            8  4  6
     3  9          – 2  0  3
+ 1  6  8          ─────────
─────────

─────────
```

The significance of the relationship between the hundreds and the tens was rarely mentioned; only that the pattern of calculating with Tens and Units could be applied here also.

Now, it must be remembered that the teacher who taught her children in this way taught very conscientiously to fulfil the demands of the school. In the infants' department, many children learned to perform these arithmetical calculations correctly by learning to remember the teacher's phrases. When this method continued throughout the school, however, there could be much misery and distress for many children.

This method depends on children memorizing correctly and children with efficient memories learned to do arithmetic. They learned to use the four operations of addition, subtraction, multiplication and division. They could perform correctly as long as the teacher revised often and gave them a lot of practice. Those were the days of working through an arithmetic textbook from page 1 to the end and doing perhaps forty examples each day. The lesson was largely one of silence with children's heads bowed over their jotters.

By the end of the primary school, some children had become speedy, efficient human calculators. There were other children, however, who had not been able to remember the facts and operations from the beginning. Arithmetic is a progressive subject and so these children became increasingly bewildered as more and more facts were showered upon them. Many of them simply closed their minds to arithmetic and considered themselves 'failures'.

Even the most conscientious, imaginative teacher knew she had these children in her class. She knew her method of telling the children how to perform an operation, waiting until the class had memorized it and then practised it, was not 100 per cent successful. She knew that many of her children were learning a 'mumbo-jumbo' and then applying it.

In subtraction, for example, the method of equal additions was in vogue and the unison chorus of children dealing with the following example might have been any of these:

$$\begin{array}{ccc} H & T & U \\ 3 & 4 & 2 \\ -1 & 8 & 6 \\ \hline \\ \hline \end{array}$$

(a) '6 from 2 I cannot; add a 10 to the top and a 10 to the bottom.'
(b) '. . .; 10 up, 10 down.'
(c) '. . .; borrow a ten and pay back.'
(d) '. . .; add 1 to the top and 1 to the bottom.'

The obvious flaw in this method of authoritarian class teaching was that the children were performing calculations in arithmetic without any understanding of number. They were simply manipulating digits.

The child who has learned to multiply decimal fractions by 'moving the point', who multiplies by 100 by 'adding two os', who divides vulgar fractions by 'inverting the divisor and multiplying', may reach a correct solution when the problem remains familiar, but he does not need to think, he simply responds to a stimulus.

Teachers began to feel unhappy about this class teaching. They knew they should be giving greater scope to the children who wanted to think about number and they were sorry for the less able children who were lost.

The method of group teaching, therefore, became popular with many teachers. The class was subdivided for the arithmetic lesson into perhaps three, or even four groups. The clever children worked as a group at their own quick pace, the slower children at their own pace, and so on.

This method meant that each group of pupils could work at the level which suited it. The teacher still taught facts and operations—not to the whole class as previously, but to a group which was ready. This meant that no longer was there one class textbook. One group might be using Book 4 of the series while another used Book 3 or even Book 2.

There were three important results of group teaching. First, the arithmetic attainment tests fell into disuse since the child's age had no longer a bearing on his computational skill. Secondly, each child was now able to feel a sense of achievement at his own level of ability. The able children were no longer bored by continual repetition and the less able were no longer being rushed along in a meaningless whirl. Perhaps the third result is the most significant, however. Children who learn to work in groups learn to work independently since the teacher is not telling them what to do all the time. They become self-reliant. When they finish their assignment of work, they seek extra work to do. In short, they develop an attitude to work which stems from their own independence.

The next stage in the development of arithmetic was prompted, therefore, by the children themselves. They began to question the work they were doing. They began to read books about number apart from their textbook. They asked for help to understand what they were learning. As one child asked: 'Why should it be that when I add 5 and 5 and 5 and 5 it's not only the same answer as 4 times 5, it's the same answer as 5 times 4?'

The need for structural apparatus was apparent and the later part of the 1950s saw the introduction of new materials into many schools.

The energy of Dr Caleb Gattegno ensured that teachers heard about Cuisenaire rods. Number relationships were discovered and seen by children using these coloured wooden rods. Professor Dienes' Multibase Arithmetical Blocks reinforced children's understanding of place value. 'Unifix' material, Catherine Stern's apparatus and others all found a ready market at this time.

Teachers began to talk about making number meaningful to children and many educationists had an influence on the teaching of arithmetic. Leonard Sealey with his *Creative Use of Mathematics* did much to help teachers to see that when children are given the opportunity to use materials, they learn and understand about simple mathematics.

The formal progression of arithmetic which had been in vogue for so long was:

Composition and decomposition of 10.
The four rules of addition, subtraction, multiplication and
    division.
The four rules in money.
Tables of length, weight, capacity and time.
The four rules with these.
Vulgar fractions.
Simple problems
    ('Plowden Report'—*Children and their Primary Schools*).

Teachers were now finding that when children were given the opportunity to work in groups using structured material of some kind, their learning did not always follow the progression set down in many schemes of work.

The traditional scheme of work which detailed exactly what should be done in each class became an obsolete document. Teachers guided their pupils to do what they were capable of doing based on a real understanding (at last) of number and number relationships.

The old arithmetic book with its hundreds of examples to labour through became an anachronism. Children who had been led to an understanding of some number process did not need to practise forty examples daily. They needed practice only to consolidate their understanding.

Teachers turned to the new books which began to appear in great number. These books were written in a more exciting way. No longer were there pages and pages of graded arithmetic examples. Children were being asked to find out for themselves—to find out by doing. They were being asked to think about number and also about their environment with its weights and measures, its money and time, its shapes.

This was the world of the mid-twentieth century—the age of mathematics—the computer age—the space age. No longer did the word 'mathematics' seem an irrelevance in the primary school. The need for understanding and knowing about mathematics had arrived.

Another need was apparent in daily life—people who were thinking and adaptable; able to transfer their learning to new situations. No longer was the standard answer to the standard question sufficient.

Many teachers were made aware of this and the pattern of teaching arithmetic evolved into one of primary mathematics. Groups of pupils were now working from a primary mathematics book, extra work cards, supplementary books and apparatus for learning to understand about number, measurement and shape. The teacher's rôle had assumed that of guide and helper as much as teacher, keeping a watchful eye on the progress of each group.

The deathly silent classroom had become a more active, less tense environment. A freer relationship came to exist between teacher and pupils. Group and class discussions became a part of the classroom scene.

Many teachers welcomed this relaxation in the rigidity of the classroom situation. They welcomed the fresh air blowing away the cobwebs of an unrealistic content. They welcomed the newer topics of shape and pattern in number. There were some teachers, however, who were worried in case their newer approach would mean 'a lowering of standards'. These teachers needed help and reassurance. No longer did they have the security of a scheme of work. No longer could they rely on a textbook to see the progression of their pupils' work.

Much of the help and inspiration given to teachers at this time was from Edith Biggs, H M I, who worked tirelessly with teachers throughout the country. Her enthusiasm was matched only by her skill and she succeeded in proving to many teachers that every child should experience what A. N. Whitehead called 'the joy of discovery'. She had teachers themselves working in an exciting, stimulating environment at her many courses. There, they too, were able to experience this joy and they began to see mathematics in a new light. They had learned as pupils by rote learning, now they were learning—and understanding —by doing.

The impact made by Miss Biggs was felt in classes throughout the country. Assignment cards appeared in profusion and the rather rigid groups of pupils seen previously began to give way to a more flexible situation with smaller groups of children and more stimulating mathematical discovery work.

All this meant that a visit to a good classroom in the 1960s would have shown children actively involved in their own learning. The classroom was a place of stimulation with a relaxed atmosphere and a happy relationship between pupils and teacher. The latter had had to learn to know when to step in and teach, and when it was better for her to remain outside the group. This was a new skill which some teachers were happy to learn.

There were also teachers, however, whose method of teaching had not changed. Their rôle was still that of the authoritarian class teacher. Some people found they could adapt to changes although they might not necessarily see the need for them. Other people found they could not adapt to changes because their personality would not release them from the security of teaching in the way which was familiar to them.

Whether teachers were avant-garde or reactionary, one could not fail to see that there was a need for a programme of some kind which would help them to see a progression in the mathematics work being done by their children: 'What does one lead a child on to after he has discovered that triangles are rigid?', 'What should an infant be expected to know about solid shapes?'

Teachers need to know the content of their work and they need to know also what the progression could be. The many new mathematics books did not satisfy these needs.

In 1964, therefore, Dr Geoffrey Matthews was asked by the Director of the Nuffield Foundation to consider a project for Junior Mathematics. He formed a team with five other educational experts. They discarded the idea of a scheme of work and decided to write Guides for teachers. It was stated:

The aim of the Nuffield Junior Mathematics Project is to devise

C.A.S.—6

a contemporary approach for children from 5 to 13. The stress
is on how to learn not on what to teach. Running through all
the work is the central notion that the children must be free to
make their own discoveries and think for themselves, and to
achieve understanding instead of learning off mysterious drills.

This was a tremendous task which was undertaken by Dr
Matthews and his team. Some of these Guides have been published and some are at present being written. They are some
of the most exciting books to reach the primary school in recent
years. Their influence has been seen and felt far beyond the
original 14 pilot areas in the project and the Chinese proverb
which was chosen as the motto is being acted upon by teachers
everywhere.

> I hear and I forget,
> I see and I remember,
> I do and I understand.

The work of Professor Piaget of Geneva is acknowledged in the
Teachers' Guides.

> Children acquire mathematical concepts much more slowly
> than we realized. They learn by their own activities.
> Although children think and reason in different ways, they
> pass through certain stages depending on their chronological and
> mental ages and their experience.

These Guides are helping teachers to see this and, in addition,
they are giving a suggested line of progression in the three main
topics 'Computation and Structure', 'Shape and Size' and
'Pictorial Representation'.

The teacher who sees her children acquiring mathematical
concepts through the experiences and opportunities contrived
in the exciting classroom is convinced that this is the way in
which her children will learn most readily.

There has thus been a gradual evolution in both method and
content from the days of a class of children sitting silently at
narrow desks, heads down over the arithmetic jotters, to the
modern primary school.

Change is in the very life blood of educational progress but
only a gradual change is a good change. The teacher who

revolutionizes her method of teaching overnight causes unhappiness among her pupils and to herself. Wisely, there has been a very gradual evolution in the teaching of mathematics in the primary schools.

When one uses the word 'mathematics' in connection with the primary school today, one wants to give children 'a knowledge and appreciation of mathematics as a creative subject; a knowledge of its order and pattern; a realization that it is present in everyday life and in the environment' (Edith Biggs). This is needed in the age of mathematics in which we live. Children need also to be able to calculate efficiently.

Let us consider in some detail how this new approach to teaching and learning is evolving.

At the beginning of the child's school life the teacher goes very slowly. She knows that her pupils are still at a level of development at which they learn from experiences gained through activity. The teacher knows also that mathematical concepts are developed from practical experiences.

The child enters school, therefore, into a play situation. There is no difference between work and play to the young child. They are one and the same. The teacher observes the child's behaviour as he plays with sand, water, clay, building bricks, a shop, a house, woodwork, dressing up and all the other activities one sees in a good infant classroom. These play activities, with reading activities, occupy most of the school day and in them relationships of many kinds are experienced.

The growth of the language of relationships is stimulated by the teacher talking with the children at play—big, bigger, small, smaller, longer, taller, shorter, heavy, light, many, few, are some of the words and ideas learned in this way. The child's ability to communicate and his knowledge of language have always been considered essential for the teaching of reading, but only recently has the teacher fully realized that it is the beginning of mathematics too. This is seen very clearly by watching and listening to children in these play activities.

Another important aspect of these is the method of learning which emerges. Concentration, thought and experimentation are needed by these young children and thus their whole attitude to learning can be encouraged.

If a teacher observes no natural progression in the children's mathematical learning, then she may contrive situations to encourage it. A possible progression in the realm of number is described below.

The basic activity of *sorting* objects into different sets may be a contrived situation where the child is asked to sort out a box containing a few shells, beads, matchboxes and buttons, into sets. They may then be led on to more particular sorting where they separate similar objects according to certain criteria—for example, separating beads into different colours, ribbons into different lengths, etc.

Matching is another basic activity used frequently in the early stages. The teacher who wants her children to appreciate the conservation of number, gives them many experiences of matching a straw to each bottle, one cup with one saucer, etc. This experience of 'one-to-one correspondence' helps children at a later stage to establish that 'five is always five'. We taught many children previously to repeat such phrases as 'five and five are ten' without realizing that they had not yet established the concept of conservation of number.

Once this has been established, the teacher encourages the child to learn about number to 10. He learns the sequence of the numbers to 10, the numerals from 0–10 and he learns to write these. He learns to match the appropriate numeral to the correct number. For example,

$$\bullet \quad \bullet \quad \bullet \quad \bullet \qquad \boxed{4}$$

When he is finding out about these numbers, he is guided to group objects and regroup them to see how numbers can be combined:

```
o o o        o o        o o
o o o        o o         o
             o o        o o o
  6           6          6
```

4 and 2 are 6,
2 and 2 and 2 are 6,
5 and 1 are 6.

The children are led to add and also to subtract with numbers to 10. Children discover these very readily since in all their number work there is material at hand—shells, buttons, bricks, etc.

Some children want to record their number work and in time they are guided to the stage when they practise their new skill by using a simple card. The child knows he can count. He wants to do sums.

$$4+3=7$$
$$2+5=7$$
$$6+1=7$$
$$0+7=7$$

So far the child has been a unitary counter—he has counted on and counted back in ones. The teacher may now encourage him to see a relationship between numbers by giving him Cuisenaire rods or a similar apparatus which aids the discovery of number relationships and discourages unitary counting.

He then builds up and break downs number within 20 and discovers for himself many number facts. For example, one child wrote down the following 'discoveries' about 12:

$8+4=12,$	$12-8=4,$	$12 \div 4=3,$	$\frac{1}{3} \times 12=4,$
$4+8=12,$	$12-4=8,$	$12 \div 3=4,$	$\frac{1}{4} \times 12=3,$
$9+3=12,$	$12-9=3,$	$12 \div 6=2,$	$\frac{1}{2} \times 12=6.$
$3+9=12,$	$12-3=9,$	$12 \div 2=6,$	
$3 \times 4=12,$			
$4 \times 3=12.$			

The teacher realizes that in order to learn and understand numbers from 20 to 100, the child has to study these in considerable depth. Unless he understands how these numbers are built up and related, his work later will become a meaningless manipulation of digits. At this stage the child is given experiences which lead him to an understanding of place value and its implications.

Often the teacher underestimated the child's difficulty with place value and so, today, she gives some direct guidance on this. A typical assignment may read:

Make each of these numbers on your abacus card:
11, 10, 19, 24, 39, 50.
Add 2 to each of them and then record your new number.

The child takes 19, for example, and on his abacus card he indicates it thus:

T	U
	o o
	o o
o	o o
	o o
	o

He then adds 2 units as directed.
He finds he has 10 and 1 in the units column.
He changes his ten units for a ten and puts
　　that in the tens column.

His abacus card then shows:

T	U
o	
	o

These are extended to H T U when the child has appreciated that Tens are Units × 10 and Hundreds are Tens × 10.

Dienes' Multi-base Arithmetical Blocks give children an understanding of place value by helping them to work not only in base 10 but in other bases too.

From a broad study of numbers to 100, using Dienes' M A B, a number line, number squares and any other available material, the four operations of addition, subtraction, multiplication and division, emerge. Children find their own methods of performing these operations. They may not be the most efficient methods but ones which are meaningful to the child. There will be discussion of the various methods used. After this the teacher may introduce the conventional methods to the children for efficiency and compactness.

An example of children learning to record the operation of addition is given below. The teacher posed the question:

> John had 27 marbles. In his first game he won 13 and in his second game he won another 4. How many marbles has he altogether?

Children dealt with this in several different ways.

(i) 2 tens and 1 ten→3 tens (ii) $27+10=37$
     7 and 3 and 4→14 $37+3=40$
     30 and 10 and 4→44; $40+4=44;$

(iii) $20+10+7+3+4=20+10+10+4=44.$

These show a clear understanding of addition. The children have appreciated place value.

As with addition, children are given freedom to devise their own ways of subtracting. For example,

Anne had a packet with 57 sweets in it. We ate 28 of them. How many had Anne left?

Children's methods were:

(i) $57-28.$ (ii) $57-20=37,$
      Well $58-28=30,$ $37-\ 7=30,$
      so $57-28=29;$ $37-\ 8=29;$

(iii) 28 and 2→30,
       30 and 27→57,
       so 28 and 29→57.
       She had 29 left.

Multiplication:

There are 5 boxes in the cupboard. In each box there are 16 pencils. How many pencils are there altogether?

(i) $2\times16=32,$ (ii) $5\times10→50,$
      $4\times16=64,$ $5\times6→30,$
      so $5\times16=64+16=80;$ $5\times16→50+30→80;$

(iii) 16   (iv) $8\times5=40,$
       16                  $16\times5=80.$
       16
       16
     + 16
     ─────
       80

Just as multiplication is regarded by the children as repeated addition so, too, does division seem to be repeated subtraction.

Many children would subtract fours in order to solve the problem:

How many boys could each get 4 biscuits from a box containing 24 biscuits?

When the teacher guides her children to the usual methods of recording these operations she will be building on the experience and understanding which have gone before.

The child who has succeeded in working with number to 100 in this way is led on to experiences greater than 100, and his learning built on this approach helps him to develop a real understanding of our whole decimal number system.

When children want to record some facts or communicate information, they may do this by means of a graph. An infant

OUR BIRTHDAY CHART

class had a chart about birthdays. This provided much discussion and some children wanted to write about it (see p. 78).

Older children, who enjoy collecting information, often make a graph of their own. The one below was made by a 9-year-old child.

His writing was a spontaneous activity after he had compiled his facts.

🐕	Dog	XXXXXXXXXX
🐱	Cat	XXXX
🐹	Hamster	X
🐹	Guinea pig	XXXXX
🐰	Rabbit	XXX
🐭	Mouse	XXX
🐢	Tortoise	X
🐦	Canary	X
🦜	Budgerigar	XXXXXXXXXX
🐟	Goldfish	XXXXXXXXXXXXXXXXXXXXXXXXXXXXX
🐠	Tropical Fish	XXXXXXXXXXXXXXXXXXX

GRAPH SHOWING PETS KEPT AT HOME

We have more goldfish than any other pets. There are 29.
   $29 = 2 \times 14 + 1$
There are ten dogs and four cats $10 + 4 = 14$
There is one tortoise and two mice $2 - 1 = 1$
There are five guinea pigs. There used to be six but one died.
   $6 - 1 = 5$
There are twenty-nine goldfish and eighteen tropical fish and eleven budgies $29 + 18 + 11 = 58$
I can do that a different way
$2 \times 14 + 2 \times 9 + 2 \times 5 + 2 = 58$
We did something horibil. We missed our mice and hamster but onr hamster died. We had only one hamster.

The teacher encourages personal research in this way but she is also conscious of her rôle and she guides children to learn about bar graphs, line graphs, ready reckoner graphs, conversion graphs, etc., so that the most suitable graphs will be used in the relevant situation.

The development of a child's understanding of measures is slow and again practical experience is given to children. It must be purposeful and progressive, and so the teacher guides it from the child experiencing measures in the play situation. There he experiences and develops an understanding of relationships—long(er), short(er), heavy, heavier, more, less, etc. Gradually the child progresses to using various convenient units—spans, paces, marbles, jars, spoonfuls, etc. He finds these unsatisfactory and sees the need for standard units. These are then introduced. In this way the child builds up an understanding of measures—and a better appreciation of them than was traditionally gained (see Plate IX).

Children are made aware of shapes in the world around them both in the world of nature and in man-made structures. They are given the opportunity to investigate and explore spatial relationships just as they do number relationships. From an early age, children are aware of shapes as they make junk models, sort different shapes and explore widely (see Plates VII and VIII).

Some examples of the type of assignments which children might undertake in order to establish an understanding of area are given in the following extract from the Nuffield Junior Mathematics Teachers' Guide *Shape and Size*, 2.

Provide a set of books of the same shape and size (e.g. exercise books).

Estimate the number of books you will need to cover the top of the table, so that the books do not overlap. Then fit the books on to the table top to cover it. How many did you use? How near was your estimate?

(Similar activities with dusters, sheets of newspaper, used postage stamps on surfaces of various sizes. Let children suggest which they should use, e.g. stamps for small surfaces such as bookcovers, newspaper for large surfaces such as corridors, or floors in classroom.)

Provide sets of geometrical shapes made of plastic material, or card. These should include squares, rectangles, regular triangles, regular hexagons, regular pentagons, circles, with a sufficient number of each of the same size to try to cover the surfaces to be investigated.

Take all the triangles. Estimate how many you will have to use to cover the front of the large reading book. Then use the triangles to cover your book. How many did you use? Was your estimate too big, or too small?

Repeat with the other shapes, i.e. use only circles, hexagons, rectangles, and so on.

With which of these shapes did you find you could cover a surface?
Which were not very good for this purpose?
Write about this in your own way.

Give children several books (or similar shapes) with covers of different area.

Arrange these books in order of size by the surface of front cover.
Which is biggest, which is smallest?
Write about how you did it.

Note whether children compare by using units to cover each, or by placing books on each other thus:

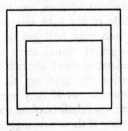

Compare the area (amount of surface) of various shapes using a grid, e.g. chicken wire. This has spaces roughly hexagonal in shape. Table mats, postcards, books, any flat objects with an interesting irregular shape are useful for this work.

Children might be set this task:

> Take three of these shapes. Use the wire netting to find which has the biggest surface on one side. Tell your teacher how you did it and write and draw about it.

Some eight-year-olds in one school were moving from one classroom to another. The desks were being carried by eleven-year-olds. A discussion arose as to whether they would have enough room to arrange the desks in groups of three, or whether they would have to be arranged in rows. One eight-year-old boy said, 'They will still take up the same space, because it doesn't matter which way you put them, each desk will still cover the same space on the floor.'

From this remark they started work on comparing areas of the corridor. The teacher provided sheets of newspaper and the children found their own way of comparing areas.

This is the time to discuss with the children various ways of covering a surface they have used so far.

E.g. 'Let's look at all the things we've used for finding which of these has the biggest area.' (Triangles, squares, circles, wire netting, etc.) 'Which do you think were useful?'

Discussion should lead to the idea of using squares, triangles, regular hexagons; and why pentagons, circles are not as useful. By analogy with the use of the cube for 3D space the square is probably the most useful. At this stage areas will be measured by the number of standard squares required to cover them and estimates must be made of the odd bits at the boundary of the surface covered. Children may well get on to the idea of taking two odd bits which together would seem to have just about the same area as the standard square; alternatively, they could get a reasonable approximation by ignoring the 'small' odd bits and counting the 'large' ones in as if they were each covered by a standard square. Much useful discussion could arise over various methods of approximating if these are suggested by the children.

Some assignments using squares can now be given.

Provide some tracing paper marked in squares ($\frac{1}{2}$ in, $\frac{3}{4}$ in, or 1 in will do).

Cover the front of your book with the squared paper and find out how big it is by counting squares. Now do the same on a different book cover. Which was bigger? How do you know?

Use graph paper marked in $\frac{1}{2}$ in, $\frac{3}{4}$ in or 1 in squares in a similar way. Trace round regular shapes and compare areas.

Then try it on irregular shapes such as leaves using the square grid on the tracing paper.

When a group has done this discuss with them what to do with the bits of squares round the edge of the shapes.

Other activities:

Draw round the sole of your shoe on the squared paper. When your group have all done this find out whose shoe covers up the biggest surface on the paper.

Provide paper with squares on one side only.

Draw an animal on the plain side of the paper. Cut it out. Turn it over and compare it with the animals of the others in your group. Find out who has the animal with the biggest area. Arrange all of the cut-outs in order of area, biggest first, smallest last. Write about what you did in your group.

A frieze of these, or leaves, could be made for a wall display.

Can you use the squared paper to find the surface area of this tin? (or other cylindrical object.)

Provide a box with lid, e.g. a chalk box, and a cylindrical tin or container, e.g. a salt drum.

See if you can find which of these has the larger outside surface area. You may use the squared paper to help you.

Larger squares of cardboard, or hardboard, can be used for comparing large surfaces such as desk tops, the tops of low cupboards and so on. Classroom floor areas can be measured and compared by counting tiles or wood floor blocks.

Primary mathematics has broadened the whole picture of mere number in the primary school and today there is a closer liaison between the primary school and the secondary school mathematics department. This has meant the introduction of some new topics and there is an increasing amount being done with sets, relations, mappings, flow charts, etc. This may be termed as simply 'tasting' mathematical topics but whether these are learned in depth or not seems immaterial in the primary school.

The important point is that primary-school children who are being guided in a progressive way by their teacher through this development of mathematics have a greater chance of becoming thinking, articulate, adaptable people whose understanding of mathematical principles is sure.

'Mathematics' is no longer an amusing, absurd word in connection with the primary school. Today it is relevant, enjoyable and desperately vital.

FOR FURTHER READING

Mathematics in Primary Schools, Curriculum Bulletin No. 1, H.M.S.O., 1965.

Nuffield Junior Mathematics Project: *I do and I understand, Pictorial Representation, Beginnings, Mathematics Begins, Shape and Size, Computation and Structure*, Chambers and Murray, 1967.

Association of Teachers of Mathematics, *Notes on Mathematics in Primary Schools*, Cambridge University Press, 1967.

Sealey, L. G. W., *The Creative Use of Mathematics*, Blackwell, (6 vols.) 1961–63.

Churchill, E., *Counting and Measuring*, Routledge and Kegan Paul, 1961.

Isaacs, N., *New Light on Children's Ideas of Number*, Ward Lock, 1962.

Barnett, N. M., Faithfull, M. G., and Theakston, T. R., *Juniors Learning Mathematics*, Ward Lock, 1962.

Land, F., *Language of Mathematics*, Murray, 1960.

Lovell, K., *The Growth of Basic Mathematical and Scientific Concepts in Children*, U.L.P., 1961.

7. Science

F. F. Blackwell

IT IS about a hundred years since 'object lessons' first appeared on the school timetables. These were devoted to descriptions of a variety of things. Some were related to the child's experience, but many were quite outside its range. The good teacher tried to make the lessons more real with drawings on the blackboard, by displaying pictures from suitable books or by having some vaguely related objects in the classroom. These were held up for the pupils to see as the lesson went on. There were lessons on camels, the ostrich, wheat, railways, clocks, the voice, canals, glaciers and the Battle of Waterloo. These subjects were only described by the teacher, the pupils listening and answering a question now and again during the lesson. There were Object Lesson Books from which the teacher prepared the work. These gave facts to pass on to the pupils, illustrations for the blackboard and suggestions for the plan of the lesson. Usually there were sufficient topics for two lessons each week for the class during the school year.

In about 1895, Inspectors of Schools were commenting on the fact that object lessons, whilst giving interesting information, neither cultivated the habit of obtaining knowledge directly and at first hand, nor developed the faculty of observation. One report said 'if the children have no opportunity of handling or watching the actual object which is being dealt with, the teacher will be giving an information lesson rather than an object lesson. It should always be remembered that in object lessons the imparting of information is secondary to the cultivation of the faculty of observation'. So a change in emphasis came about, teachers chose topics which could be developed from a study of an actual specimen. The common flora of the locality, common animals and common subjects of interest were listed as topics for study. The oldest pupils had

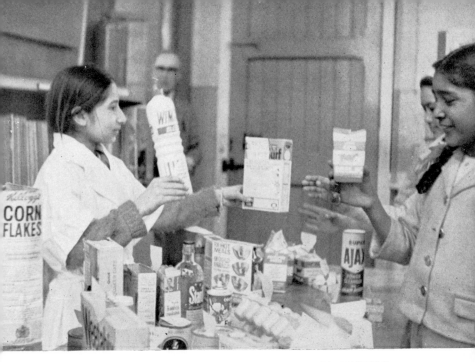

ENGLISH FOR NON-ENGLISH-SPEAKING PUPILS

I

(above) *'Would you like this one or that one?'* Dialogues in the class shop provide practice of a new structural pattern.

II

(left) *'Is this a bus or a car?'* . . . A simple language game with picture cards.

FRENCH

III A performance of a puppet play using home-made puppets and scenery. In the background a part of the 'French Corner'.

IV Children use cut-outs to develop confidence in using question and answer forms.

V

Shopping situations give real meaning to the language the children are learning.

SOCIAL STUDIES

VI

An altar painting designed by children from a mining community.

MATHS

VII Project work.

VIII Constructing polyhedra with straws.

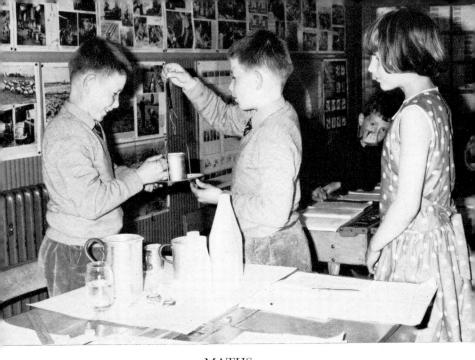

MATHS

IX Practical weights and measures.

X Discovering some properties of circles.

SCIENCE

XI Finding the speed of sound.

XII A corner for practical work.

XIII

St George and the Dragon: a paper mosaic by a ten-year-old boy.

XIV Cats: a drawing by a ten-year-old girl.

DRAMA

XV 'Watch out for bandits!'

SPREADING THE NEW IDEAS

XVI At the teachers' centre.

lessons on coal-gas, iron, tin, zinc, matches, effect of heat upon bodies, water, the barometer, the common pump and so on. In effect, simple science topics began to emerge as the core of material for object lessons. History and geography appeared as subjects on the timetable and embodied some of the suitable topics from the list of earlier object lessons.

The process of curriculum change went on slowly, with much 'nature study' being taught to the younger children whilst simple chemistry and physics was given to the older pupils. Thus the pattern of elementary school science in the first thirty years of this century became established. The presence of actual specimens began to be supported by demonstration lessons by the teacher, to reinforce particular points. This was usually done with topics in physics and chemistry. We were still a long way short of science teaching as we now think of it.

In 1926 the Hadow Report proposed the division of schools into those providing for children up to the age of 11 and those which would cater for children from 11 to school-leaving age, which was then 14. Broadly this established the present pattern of primary and secondary education. At once came the problem of providing a suitable curriculum for each stage to replace the previous curriculum designed for single schools catering for the whole age-range of 5 to 14 years. A solution was found by allocating the nature study material, mainly elementary botany and zoology, to the lower age groups; whilst retaining the elementary physics and chemistry and some biology for pupils in the upper schools.

This nature study was mainly descriptive and retained some of the flavour of the object lesson. The material was drawn from the common flora and fauna of the area. Collecting specimens was encouraged and the inclusion of observations on the weather was a common feature of many syllabuses. Children were expected to make their own notes of their observations and to record the names of specimens. The teacher still acted as the main provider of information, though usually there was a class textbook which gave additional help to the pupil, particularly with the writing of notes.

In about 1953 the process of change, which led to the present situation, began. It was felt by a few educators that observation in itself was not enough, if the real objectives of science were to be served. They advocated that science, as a way of working and thinking, needed to be established as such even in the primary school, and that the existing material of nature study should be supplemented by relevant work in simple physical science. The material of the existing curriculum was not to be set aside but to be used differently.

The underlying theme of the object lesson—observation at first hand—was preserved. It was, however, not to be viewed as the end-point of work in science, but rather as one of the principal means. Children would still observe at first hand, but so as to gain evidence with which to justify their tentative conclusions. They would use observation to sharpen their natural curiosity, and so begin to ask relevant questions themselves rather than rely solely upon their teachers. Here were the seeds of great change.

By the mid-twentieth century most schools were in urban areas and rural schools were closing. Much of the syllabus material in nature study, however, remained from the time when most schools were in or near rural environments. Material which was easily available for first-hand observation then, was no longer immediately accessible to many schools. To meet this position and to provide situations and materials which lent themselves readily to first-hand investigation by the child, selected aspects of physical science were introduced.

This movement for change was not a co-ordinated one. It emerged against a background of general educational advance and arose first in the schools where the innovators were working. By 1957 the situation had developed sufficiently for the then Ministry of Education to call a conference of those concerned with science in the primary school. At the conference the diverse threads of this development were drawn together and the common use of the 'discovery' method was seen to give a unity to the work and objectives of those taking part.

Such methods, of course, demanded a freer arrangement within the classroom and it was fortunate that at this time there was a general movement in the direction of a less rigid time-table and a more informal use of resources.

Some of the innovators were committing their ideas to paper

in the form of textbooks for children. These continued to give information, but now introduced additional material drawn mainly from simple physical science. Furthermore, the texts aimed to give information which would cause children to ask questions and to see relationships. It took the purely observational situation a stage further. The biological work was in the main reshaped to bring in material for the town school. Tree studies centred on the trees of the parks and school grounds, animal studies were based upon common invertebrates of the urban area or small mammals that could be kept at home or in school.

This movement to give science a new significance in the primary school raised many questions for the teacher. Few studied science during their training. Many women teachers had little background of science in their own school-days—and primary schools were staffed mainly by women. In some ways there was as much need for teacher help as pupil support.

The B.B.C. Schools Service contributed to this advance in science teaching. Its series 'Junior Science' came in 1961 just at the time when teachers and children needed the help and stimulus that it gave. The series was designed to stimulate practical work by the pupils both during and after the broadcasts. The programmes were popular with teachers and children and opened the way for later advances.

This movement was a new experience to teachers who, along with the children, were meeting the material for the first time, and they asked 'What is science in this context?' Most teachers had thought of it first as a body of knowledge, yet now it was visualized somewhat differently. Science was presented as a way of working, through the process of problem-solving and on the basis of personal discovery. This was emphasized not only by the new books being published, by the B.B.C. series and the numerous courses for teachers arranged by local education authorities, but also by the teacher's own thinking about child development.

Primary school children are essentially empiricists and an adequate curriculum in science would develop and expand this natural attribute by exposing them to a variety of experiences. Science in this context is essentially a first-hand process of the child solving genuine problems of significance to himself and relevant to his interests and attributes. Most often it uses experiment and observation and the associated thought-process. Whilst much of this 'discovery work' is, in fact, 'rediscovery', this does not mean that the impact of its 'first timeness' for the child need be diminished. This child-based experimental approach is in great contrast with the older style teacher-based object lesson and later nature study lessons which were restricted to observation and formal teaching only.

It quickly became apparent that the rôle of the teacher would need to change if this problem-solving approach were to be adopted. No longer would old teaching methods suffice, no longer would a curriculum made up of isolated topics treated descriptively meet the needs. A different organization within the classroom, as well as equipment for the work itself would be required.

One objective at this time was to base practical work upon the use of everyday things. Teachers rightly argued that the first priority was that the child should understand the problem, and should not be confused by unfamiliar and complicated apparatus. It was urged, therefore, that, in the search for a solution to problems, use should be made of available materials and of improvization. The sophisticated scientific apparatus used in secondary schools was recognized as having little relevance in the primary sphere. Encouraging younger children to devise apparatus was seen to be one of the aims of science teaching. Thus teachers were not faced so much with problems of equipment, but with those relating to educational philosophy and outlook.

A very significant pattern emerged as more and more children began this work. Most were inspired by a problem highlighted by the teacher or by a situation contrived within the classroom. From this, the problem-solving suggestions were developed, often by means of a class discussion. Then individually, or more often in groups, children experimented to test the suggestions. Usually this exciting stage produced such stimulation that the communication of results was a natural outcome.

The purpose of communication in this context was recognized as having wide implications, first in a general educational sense with all that it implied in terms of literacy; and secondly as a vital part of the process of science. In this latter connection three aspects of its use stood out. There was communication to facilitate the further testing of suggestions for possible answers and to pose new problems or to lead to new fields of discovery. Secondly, to communicate results so that others might repeat the procedures and compare their results with those previously obtained. Thirdly, communication gave permanence, and often purpose and form, to children's work. It created the conditions for subsequent thought, questioning and experimentation and occasionally an opening for new interpretations of results. Teachers recognized the value of the urge to communicate that is liberated by practical work in science. However, it was still being interpreted rather narrowly in many schools where the patterns of note-making handed down from the previous era still lingered.

Several important national bodies concerned with science education began to take an active interest in the developments in the primary school. The British Association for the Advancement of Science organized a national conference for Inspectors, College of Education lecturers and local education authority officials. The Association for Science Education formed a Primary Science Committee and in 1963 the Nuffield Foundation established the Junior Science Project.

The aim of this project was to ensure that primary school science should not only be 'good science' but that it should fit naturally into an enlightened primary school curriculum.

When science is used in this dual sense it becomes an educational tool of great effectiveness, for it begins the development of the most powerful way of thinking and working that man possesses. It is the way that has led to the present, so-called, 'Scientific age'.

The educational effectiveness of science depends considerably upon the power and significance of the points from which it stems. The most fruitful ones would seem to be those rooted in the child's environment (bearing in mind always that the teacher is a powerful, and potentially the most effective, educational instrument in that environment). Work which leads to ever-widening horizons, fresh problems and produces a need to experiment reinforces the underlying aims in this sphere of education.

Though the choice of starting points must apparently be the child's, the guidance of the teacher is of paramount importance. Success does not come by merely exposing the child to the environment. Through the teacher's skill his eyes should be opened to the possibilities for investigation and the pursuit of new interests. Not the least of the teacher's tasks is the timely introduction of skills and background information to further the child's independence and achievement. The teacher steers the child towards the fruitful starting points and away from the trivial and the inappropriate by a positive emphasis and a shared interest in, and enthusiasm for, the worthwhile.

The Nuffield Project was content to present advice in general terms, but some other investigators worked to a very much more precise curriculum. Most schools, in fact seem to be steering a mid-way course, using the Nuffield approach, but relating it to rather more specific starting points centred on main themes of work. A common practice is to take Earth, Air and Water as the central themes and to develop the biological and physical science related to them at levels appropriate to the children concerned.

This use of a broad core of content enables teachers to keep their aims and educational intentions clear and presents fewer difficulties than a more fortuitous and purely opportunistic approach. (It is well realized, though, that a good teacher is always ready to set planned work aside so that children can take up unexpected educational opportunities as they arise.) In addition, this course of action makes it easier for teachers to determine their objectives both in terms of science and education.

The broad thematic background that seems most used by schools commends itself to teachers for another important reason. Teachers wish to take heed of the more recent work on child development and children's learning. Thus they realize that to be educationally successful they must constantly be aware of the 'wholeness' of the child's natural point of view. It looks over the whole range—subject divisions, which are characteristic of the adult level, are artificial, and sometimes hinder the child's learning. Thus, the teacher sees that the biological aspects of a particular situation are so brought into focus that they show up the need to think about and investigate the asociated phenomena of physical science—and, of course, vice-versa. It is not an artificial device, for it not only reflects the child and his own way of thinking and working but also the more integrated view of science which is taking place at other levels.

What is the classroom situation into which these various developments fit? The practical nature of science is not only fully accepted, but its needs are provided for even in the more formal classroom situation. The nature table has made way for a practical work area. In many classrooms this is extended to incorporate materials for practical work in mathematics as well. Because most of the work has developed round the use of everyday things, common to school and home, the specialist air of the secondary school laboratory is not present in these classrooms. In new schools either a practical work area of this sort is included in the classroom, or a larger space is shared between two or more classes (see Chapter 11).

Science has established itself as a practical activity and, as such, it has outgrown the bounds of a tightly timetabled space during the school week. Practical work needs a liberal time-table. Work in groups calls for flexibility; individual work requires freedom. We have seen that when science really grips the child, he will draw upon and practise skills which in the past have appeared on school timetables as separate entities. So we see the disappearance of the rigid timetable. The communication that results provides material for written and spoken work, for work in mathematics and expression in art and handicraft. Thus this moves very much nearer the wholeness of view which is characteristically the child's.

This wholeness of view is interpreted in some schools in terms of an integrated curriculum where subject boundaries are deliberately broken down. Themes are taken which preserve the unity of approach. Science grows out of suitable 'finding out' situations. In other schools the movement is towards an undifferentiated day where one facet of a theme develops into another as the work progresses, the teacher ensuring that a balance is kept between themes referring to time and place (history and geography) and cause and effect (science and mathematics), and that all give rise to communication in its widest forms (art and music).

There are several excellent features in this type of programming of the school day from the point of view of work in science. Because children are individuals they work at different rates, with different skills, insights and abilities. Rigid timetabling inevitably takes no account of this, whereas the freer timetable can do. It allows work to be truly that of the individual and the group, and so encourages the natural formulation of, and scientific solution to, problems. Discovery becomes a reality.

Against this background of a more flexible timetable it is easier to comment about the arrangement of furniture and the use of equipment in the modern primary school. Most classrooms are arranged so that children can sit and work in groups of threes, fours and sixes. Less and less are they all occupied on the same 'subject' at the same time. This is particularly convenient for science as the practical work area in most classrooms is limited in size. Groups of children can use this area, and then go to another part of the classroom to record their results, to read and to plan their next steps. Desks are being replaced by tables and in some classrooms storage units also form work tops and display areas. In such arrangements, whilst there is a seat for every child, there is not a desk, but a variety of working places, each suited to some aspect of the curriculum. There is usually a table or bench at which apparatus is made and a nearby stock of scrap materials from which most of it is constructed. Corridors and cloakrooms, playground areas and outside spaces, all are used for educational purposes and science studies in particular.

One may wonder how such arrangements work in the absence of rigidly ordered, teacher-dominated class discipline. In practice, when the teacher has established with the children how they can make sensible use of the facilities, then sheer interest and purposeful involvement carries the work along under its own motivation. It is this release of educational drive from within the child that commends this approach so strongly to teachers.

It may well be asked how children will acquire the techniques which they will need to follow up their interests with profit.

The key to the situation is to introduce such skills when the child is ready for, and able to use them. The place for direct teaching is when it is relevant, not in an unrelated and apparently random situation such as applied in the days of object lessons. In science there are still many occasions when direct teaching is needed and is given, for these are positive opportunities for the teacher to shape the educational situation according to its needs. Besides which, children cannot be expected to acquire all they need to know purely by discovery.

Many teachers skilfully use these teaching opportunities to guide children towards books which will give them the further information they will need. The resource areas have book displays relevant to children's work and reference lists to guide them to the library shelves. All this is part of the background control and guidance which the teacher must provide.

It can be seen that this new approach to science involves a radical change in the role of the teacher. Leadership from the front of the classroom gives way to a sensitive awareness of educational opportunities and needs. Judgement is required on when to introduce new material, open up new topics, and, above all, when to consolidate the experiences of experimentation by the addition of teacher-supplied information and ideas. These ideas will often provide springboards for further advances by the children. This type of leap-frog learning is perhaps the novel element in this work. In it, the children make the first move when they commence experimenting, the teacher is at hand to assist the learning and at the critical moment to take the lead, perhaps by giving information, supplying ideas, asking questions, calling in the help of the rest of the class and so on. The teacher takes the lead long enough to allow the children to regain their intellectual poise to take the initiative again for a fresh leap forward.

Teachers now need to provide themselves with the fullest possible background of knowledge and training in the techniques of work both indoors and out. They need to acquire the 'seeing eye' which is best done by first experiencing the 'eye-opening' process themselves. Hence many courses for teachers emphasize this practical side, by being themselves practically, and not lecture, based. All teachers during their training are given the techniques for self education and in their subsequent professional life they will be using them constantly. Science calls heavily upon these skills and teachers must be prepared to continue their own studies, often alongside the children and certainly as part of the normal preparation and follow-up work. This broader based preparation is no less a real part of the teacher's work than the minutely detailed lesson notes of years ago. Quite often manipulative skills will need to be acquired, as well as those of knowing where to find suitable references and illustrations.

One of the principal anxieties expressed by teachers concerns the breadth of work that is opened up when science is taught in this way and the vital need to see some pattern behind it all. At the child's level there is little point in pressing relationships and the way in which individual pieces of work take their place in the great integrating themes of science. These are difficult, adult concepts outside the children's scope. For teachers it is a different matter; they rightly feel the need to be aware of some of these underlying themes of which the children will be gaining subconscious experience.

Children need these experiences for the immediate satisfaction of their personal interests and for the part they play in the cumulative process of science education. In this the varied strands of experience are drawn together in the themes of science. At the end of school life some children may still be unable to appreciate these fully, but the experiences will not have been wasted, having been of value in the immediate work with which they were associated.

There have been several attempts recently to sketch out these great themes of science and so answer teachers' requests for assistance. Notable among these was the project based at the Oxford University Institute of Education. Some teachers take the following four, great, integrating themes as a basis:

1. *Concept of Matter*
   Substances in all their forms with an emphasis on (a) their variety, (b) their pattern.
2. *Concept of Relationships*
   (a) Living things—interrelationships, interdependence and interaction,

    (b) Non-living things—interaction, equilibrium and energy.

3. *Concept of Change*

    (a) Living things—variety, adaptation and evolution,

    (b) Non-living things—changing materials, changing Earth and an evolving universe.

4. *Concepts of Space and Time*

When the Nuffield Junior Science Project ended it was clear that there was still work to be done, and a continuation project was established under Schools Council auspices. This project, Science 5/13, is based on the Institute of Education at Bristol University and seeks, as one of its principal aims, to help teachers isolate their objectives in science.

Whilst this chapter is specifically concerned with science in the primary school, it is essential to mention very briefly the present setting of primary education into which it must fit. The Plowden Report, *Children and their Primary Schools*, considers the future of primary education and bases its findings on enlightened current practice and the latest researches in child development. It clearly demonstrates that a subject-centred view of primary education is no longer possible, that the rigidities of timetabling and programming of the school day must be eased to be compatible with children's needs as individuals, and that in these circumstances individuals and groups form the basic entities of school life. Recent developments in science do not run counter to any of these fundamentals. In fact, the evolution of work in science in the primary school parallels a general pattern of development in primary education.

This is all the more encouraging since it means that future, vigorous growth of science education will serve, and be served by, the general development of primary education. This is vital as no subject can exist today in isolation and, indeed, this was one thing which led to the disappearance of the object lesson.

Children in Britain today are not only surrounded by the products of technology, but are made aware of the latest achievements of science through television and radio. This not only stimulates their interest in science, but it also presents exciting possibilities for their education. The over-riding aim which all teachers share is to enable children to understand this scientific age in which they live, so that they will be at home in it, to work in it and enjoy it. This aim has inspired the changes in our primary schools. That the changes have been so far-reaching is a tribute to the teachers' concern for their children. Without doubt this need for change will continue, and one hopes that a generation of children educated to be at ease with science, will be able to face future changes with greater confidence.

To end this chapter we reproduce an account of a class project on sound which is taken from the Teachers' Guides published by the Nuffield Foundation Junior Science Project.

The children, who were aged between 9 and 10, were asked to bring to school anything which made a sound. On the following day a violin, a baby's rattle, a tin containing peas, a gramophone, and other objects were brought. These, together with a few school musical instruments, a tuning fork, and some books about sound were set out on a table. The children were interested and the teacher listened to their comments and questions as they played.

The children talked about their discoveries, then wrote down what they wanted to know about. This provided the teacher with enough information to draw up a list of topics:

1 Sounds and how they are made.
2 The pitch of sounds.
3 Amplification.
4 Transmitting sounds.
5 Sound insulation.
6 Acuteness of hearing.

There was a good supply of materials freely available to the children so that they were able not only to plan and perform their experiments, but also to display their findings.

After a brief discussion, the children chose the topics they wanted to study and formed groups based on their particular interests. Each group began by tackling a question, but looking back on this later, the teacher felt that the topics were too formal and, indeed, unnecessary. It would have been better simply to have asked the children to choose questions rather than topics.

Most of the work was done in groups, but there were periodic class discussions and occasional bursts of class activity, for example when an exciting discovery in one group commanded everyone's attention.

This is how the work of the different groups developed.

1 Sounds and how they are made

The children began by drawing up a list of as many sounds as possible and saying how each was made. They found that sounds were associated with vibration, for example, by putting sand on a drum, beating it, and watching the grains bouncing as the drumskin vibrated. The teacher also noticed that they were striking the tuning fork and then feeling the vibrating prongs. He left a jar half full of water on the table and soon Graham discovered that if he touched the surface of the water with a vibrating tuning fork, it made tiny waves.

The children were keenly interested in stringed instruments, and began to make their own. This is not surprising, since several of them played the violin, and various stringed instruments were included in the classroom display. They discovered that changing the length or the tension of a string altered the pitch of the sound it made.

While making a large harp from scrap materials, John noticed that the long wires vibrated slowly and made low notes while the short wires vibrated quickly and made high notes. He suggested to the group that the pitch depended upon the speed at which the string vibrated. The teacher introduced the word 'frequency' at this point and explained that the frequency of different notes could be measured. They now looked again at what happened as they tightened a vibrating string, and concluded that it altered the frequency.

This group made and experimented with various percussion instruments including drums, rattles, and a 'bottle xylophone'. They also recorded some common sounds and played them to the rest of the class, who were required to identify them.

2 The pitch of sounds

The children began by making stringed instruments and then followed a path very like the first group's. They experimented with strings of different materials and found in every case that the pitch rose as the string was shortened or tightened. Valerie made a simple instrument of a row of nails in a piece of wood with nylon fastened to them. Each string was made a little tighter than its neighbour. Figure 1 shows how she did this.

When one of the group suggested that the thickness of a string might affect the pitch of the note it made, Valerie's instrument was used to test the idea. Different thicknesses of string and nylon fishing line were tried.

The children soon found pictures of xylophones and asked if they could make some. The teacher provided some tubular metal and a few strips of oak, and then the children read in a book that the bars should rest on rubber or felt strips. They found strips of balsa wood quite satisfactory. They also made nail xylophones,

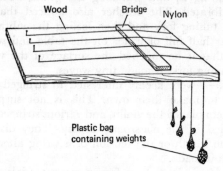

Fig. 1

but considered them unsatisfactory because the nails did not vibrate very well.

The work of the first two groups overlapped to such an extent that they gradually merged.

Paul then brought a whistling kettle to school so that everyone could hear how the pitch of the whistle rose as steam pressure built up, and this prompted two girls to write a booklet on wind instruments explaining how their recorders worked. John also wrote about a cane flute he was making and Valerie added a section about a pedal organ. This booklet was a mixture of first-hand experience and material from books.

3 Amplification

The children pursued two main lines of enquiry. The boys experimented with an old gramophone to find out how they could make the sound as loud as possible. They mounted a needle in a block of balsa and held the point in the groove of an old record on the turntable. Next they fixed the needle in the edge of a circular cheese box, then in the apex of a paper cone, and so on, until they could decide which needle holder made the most efficient amplifier. This was their own experiment which developed out of an idea they had found in a book. They found that their xylophones played louder on desks than on the floor and the teacher suggested that they should try a series of boxes. The girls began to experiment with sounding boards. They compared the sounds of a xylophone bar lying on the floor with those made when it was resting on balsa strips and on a wooden box. A boy who had been watching these experiments touched the box with a tuning fork and found that it amplified the sound. He felt sure that a bigger box would make it even louder and so collected a series of cardboard boxes to test his idea. Finally, he calculated the volume of each box.

The whole group made megaphones of different shapes and sizes and then used them as ear trumpets. Kenneth tried to explain this by saying 'They brought the sound waves to a focus'.

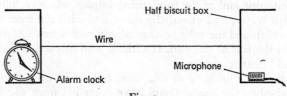

Fig. 2

They concluded their study by using tin cans to test the saying, 'Empty vessels make the most noise.'

4 Transmitting sound

The group that studied this included some of the most able children in the class. They started by making speaking-tubes from polythene funnels and rubber tubing, and when they had written descriptions of their construction and their uses, they showed them to the teacher. He felt they could take this further, and asked, 'How far will your voice carry along the tube?' They were keen to find out and tried the longest piece of rubber tubing they could find, only to discover that their voices travelled its full length. Then they made string telephones, an idea from a book, instead, and carried out some valuable experiments with different thicknesses of string and different end cups in an attempt to improve transmission.

In the junk box was some fine wire, and two children used this to make a telephone. They tried to compare the efficiency of wire and string but this was difficult until they thought of using the tape recorder. Two halves of biscuit boxes were used with a small hole in the centre of the bottom of each one. They were then placed on their sides about six feet apart and connected by a piece of wire passing through the holes, and the children put an alarm clock in one and the microphone in the other (see figure 2). They then replaced the wire by a piece of clothes-line, repeating the process until they had recorded the sound transmitted by many different strings. Finally they played the recording several times and decided which connection was best.

From a book, they got the idea of tapping the central heating pipes to see if sound would travel through metal, and it was then that Eric asked if sound travels through water. He asked the teacher for a tube to fill with water, and was given a plastic one about three feet long and an inch in diameter. He looked for corks to put in each end, but as there were none, he brought two table tennis balls and asked if he could use them. He stuck a ball into one end of the tube, using impact adhesive, filled the tube with water, and closed the other end with the second ball. He then clamped the tube horizontally, struck a tuning fork, and put it on the ball at one end. His friend who listened at the other end could hear it clearly.

The teacher said little at this time, but a day or two later he asked whether the sound could have travelled from the tuning fork to his ear without passing through the water. Eric said at once, 'Oh, of course! It could have gone along the plastic tube.'

He was determined to prove that sound could travel through water, so he used a sleigh bell and an aquarium half full of water. He held the bell under water, shook it, and pressed his ear against the glass.

Following a conversation about Red Indians listening for the sound of horses' hoofs, the children decided to find out if sound really did travel through the ground. They found a crack in the concrete playground, put the point of a long nail into it, and tapped the head with a hammer. They could hear the sound seventy-four yards away through the ground even though they could not hear it through the air.

Although most of their work involved first-hand investigation, the children loved reading and they searched in books for more information. It was hardly surprising, therefore, to find that they decided to write a booklet on modern methods of communication. It began with a brief account of the life and work of Marconi and included chapters on Morse code, semaphore, telephones, and radio.

5 Sound insulation

The group began with the question, 'How can we insulate a room from sound?' To find out what substances were good insulators, they selected a range of materials and used each, in turn, to cover an alarm clock. They measured the distance from the clock at which the sound became inaudible and presented their results as a block graph.

It was generally agreed that the sound of a transistor radio was one of the biggest nuisances in a house, so they decided to see how effectively they could insulate a room against it. They found a large cardboard box and made a compartment inside it just big enough to hold a transistor radio. The space between the compartment and the sides of the box was then packed with materials which had been found to be the most effective insulators. When the children turned on the radio and lowered it into the box, the effect was dramatic. The teacher suggested that they should take the tape recorder to the school gates and record street noises. Later, after listening to their recording, they suggested ways of reducing the noise. Amongst other things, they thought that plastic milk bottles would be a welcome innovation for those who were awakened early in the morning by the milkman.

6 Acuteness of hearing

'How do we hear?' This was the question engaging the attention of the sixth group, and they found themselves working mainly from books. They read about the human ear and drew a diagram showing its structure, then jotted a few notes about acuteness of hearing in animals. They listed the frequencies of sounds made by musical instruments and read about the range of hearing of various creatures, including humans. Some notes on bats, and how they navigate, were included.

When, near the end of term, they asked the teacher to tell them more about sound waves and what they were like, he enlisted the help of a science teacher from a nearby secondary school. He showed them a film about sound waves, and set up an oscilloscope so that they could see the trace made by their own instruments and tuning forks.

The whole class became involved when Linda announced that sound travels at 650 miles an hour. When the teacher asked how it was measured, two boys said that you had to make a sound and see how long it took to travel a mile. During the discussion which followed the teacher asked whether a firework would be of any use, and they thought it would be ideal.

The children, who can be seen in Plate XI, chose a long, straight cart track between two fields and measured a quarter of a mile. They tied a firework to the end of a long stick so that it was visible from a distance, and stood it upright. As each firework went off the children at the other end of the cart track timed the interval between seeing the flash and hearing the bang.

An extract from Linda's notes reads:

'My teacher and the boys didn't see the flash and then hear the bang. They saw the flash and heard the bang together. Because they were right under the sound. And it took less time to get to them. But we were a quarter of a mile away and it took time to reach us.

1st time $1\frac{1}{2}$ seconds.

2nd time $1\frac{1}{6}$ seconds.

3rd time $1\frac{1}{8}$ seconds.

4th time $1\frac{1}{8}$ seconds.

I think the first time when I got the result of $1\frac{1}{2}$ I wasn't quite ready. So we took the time as $1\frac{1}{8}$.'

The children timed how long it took them to walk back to school, and this was the beginning of an interest in speeds. They found out how fast they could walk, run, cycle, and skip, and then looked up the speeds of animals, birds, and aeroplanes.

Katherine read about the eruption of Krakatoa and then wrote a description of it, drawing a map showing all the places where the sound was heard. Eric rounded it off by working out the time at which the sound reached different places.

FOR FURTHER READING

Nuffield Junior Science Project, *Teachers' Guide 1, Teachers' Guide 2, Source Book. Apparatus, Source Book. Animals and Plants*, Collins, 1967.

Association for Science Education Primary Committee, *Science for Primary Schools*, Books 1–4, Murray, 1960.

Blackwell, F. F., *Starting Points for Science*, Blackwell, 1968.

8. Drama

John Allen

IT IS no accident that we use the same word for play as a play.
The process that begins when very young children dress-up
and pretend to be adults comes to a kind of fulfilment when
adults dress-up and pretend to be characters in *King Lear*.
Between one and the other an enormous range of human activity is covered; and it is increasingly clear that the vitality of
society depends upon this quality of play, whether it is
professional football or the National Theatre at one end,
or the cavortings of a group of children in the street at the
other.

This emphasis on the importance of play among children is
nothing new. It has been discussed by teachers and psychologists for more than a hundred years. But it is impossible to
write about drama without reverting to the subject since one
of the outstanding qualities of children's play is something we
can only call 'dramatic'; though it need hardly be added that
one makes the strongest possible distinction between this use
of the word and a kind of theatricality that is often associated with the work of adults.

What then do we mean by this dramatic quality of children's
play? We mean, to begin with, their deep interest in, and
instinct for, identification. A child who is running down the
street identifies himself with an aeroplane. When boys kick a
ball around in the playground they often identify themselves
with a football hero. Girls in nursery schools tend to identify
themselves with their mothers, other relatives, nurses and
teachers. Boys identify themselves with adults they wish to
emulate—sailors, firemen, engine-drivers; or characters from
their private mythology such as cops and robbers, cowboys and
Indians, and spacemen. It is clearly a profound and involuntary instinct.

The play of children must be of the greatest interest to teachers since there is no activity in which we reveal ourselves so personally. Other chapters in this book describe the way in which teachers encourage children to play with all kinds of materials so that they learn something about the nature of these materials and their relationship to abstract concepts such as weight, volume, height, and so on. In dramatic play the concepts are harder for us to recognize since they relate to feelings, ideas, relationships, and the expression of that inner imaginative life that we can only foster by helping to give it form and outward expression; but they are none the less important for children to experience.

If dramatic play is so important, what should teachers do about it apart from allowing it to take place? A frequent practice is to provide a large space filled with crates and boxes, car tyres and many other oddments which is usually taken over by the boys, and a small space in the corner of the classroom—still sometimes called the Wendy House—crammed with a dresser, sink, ironing-board, bed and chest-of-drawers, all in miniature, which is mostly used by the girls. The boys tend to do better out of this than the girls who are consigned to premature domesticity even though the boys do visit them occasionally for a cup of tea. But in schools where the importance of quality of play is understood, the teachers do their best to provide a far richer environment. Boys and girls dress up as chefs and make their own cakes; they will turn a part of the classroom into a dress shop, a museum, or a picture-gallery, filling it, when appropriate, with their own work and taking it in turns to be assistants, curators, guides, and the general public. In some schools the play of the children has been enriched by the provision of all kinds of dressing-up clothes together with crowns, helmets, swords and shields which they have made in their handwork lessons. This variety of play which hovers between the children's own ideas and the discreet suggestions of the teacher only takes place in schools where the teachers pay close attention to every aspect of the development of their children.

When children move on from infant to junior school there is little opportunity in the classroom for their own involuntary play which now takes place at break, in the playground, and after school hours; but teachers realize the importance of keeping an eye on what the children are doing, not only for disciplinary reasons, but also to observe their development and their behaviour when left absolutely to themselves. If, in the junior school, play is permitted in the classroom it is likely to be of a fairly intentioned kind, perhaps to be described as drama rather than dramatic play, though many teachers feel that this is not the word with which to describe an activity that may be at the roots of, but is still some distance from, dramatic art.

One of the important tasks of a primary school teacher is to help children to understand something about their bodies. We use our bodies, of course, in everything we do, and teachers can learn a great deal about their children from the way in which they walk, sit, run, handle pencils and paint-brushes, eat their food, and go about their play and their work. But observation is only the beginning. Teachers must develop the physical resources of their children and in so doing they often stimulate work which finds its expression in dance and drama. This emergence of a dramatic quality in movement is an interesting phenomenon since it suggests that some movement has given rise in the children to an image or imaginative idea that can only be expressed in physical form. Thus from their early identification with adults, they begin to explore the distinctive way of moving of a far wider range of human beings and animals and so into the richly imaginative world of witches, giants, dwarfs and the much loved space-monsters. All these characters are identified with, or inhabit, a situation or an environment; they involve the children in working both individually and in groups which they are able to do with the greatest sensitivity. It is a short step for children then to use words, costumes, properties and other visual symbols of the environment they have created.

Although we express ourselves socially as well as dramatically through words as well as movements, some teachers find diffi-culty in handling this part of a child's education. They recog-nize the importance of talking to children, of helping them to put their ideas, thoughts, feelings, and observations into words and of letting them realize that they are really listening to what they have to say; but they fear to make the child self-conscious about something as personal and involuntary as speech. Thus they tend to leave the development of vocal and linguistic resources to the incidental by-products of classroom discussion and work in English. This of course is no small matter. If children have plenty of opportunities to talk in a meaningful manner, if they have read to them, and if they read, plenty of stories and poetry, if they are encouraged to write freely themselves, their vocabulary and their ability to use words will increase. There is considerable evidence that drama can help children impressively in this. Indeed, it is said to be firmly established that the ability of children under five to use words is closely related to their developing powers of reasoning.

Many delightful stories are told of the inappropriateness of children's language for the situation they are depicting. The Virgin Mary refers to the infant Jesus as having been 'a proper little so-and-so' and a child from a seaside resort blamed Joseph for their being out in the cold through his 'failure to book'. Lady Macbeth tries to cheer her husband with bacon-and-eggs and a chief witch invited her minions to 'retire to their stew'. But this is all a part of the initial process of children making a situation their own. The acquisition of appropriate language comes slowly. The point to be made about drama is that it provides situations to which the child must respond through his own immediate resources. He cannot hide behind the clay, or the painting, or the poem written out in the book. The onus is on his personal powers of expression at that very moment and this seems to be a challenge which many children accept with a flow of words and an expressiveness in movement that less imaginatively demanding situations do not always produce.

On the subject of speech it is worth pointing out that the spoken language shares qualities of pitch, tempo, volume, inflection, and register with music and that teachers of languages are increasingly aware of the importance of a musical sensibility in learning to acquire the rhythms of speech. Thus in their close relationship to movement and dance, to the spoken language, and to the exploration of dramatic

situations, sound and music are a part of the total ingredients
of drama.

We should also emphasize the relationship of drama to
experience in the visual arts, though, once again, this is only
to suggest relationships with subjects that are fully described
elsewhere in this book. Drama and the visual arts are not
always brought into close contact with each other. This is
perhaps a reflection of a weakness in the practice of adult
drama. But it is certainly a weakness on the part of many
teachers that they fail to develop that propensity for dressing-up
which is so marked a feature of dramatic play in the infant
school. A skirt, a cloak, a scarf or hat, a cap or helmet, a pair
of boots or high-heeled shoes is enough to help a child change
his whole person. A single, visual symbol of identification is
enough to touch something within him of great significance.
If we developed this will to dress-up, we should help children
not only to handle a large variety of textiles and fabrics, which in
many schools they weave and dye, print and paint, but also to
relate them more closely to the clothes they wear and then to the
characters they impersonate in their drama. The relationship of
the visual arts and of handwork to drama often stops short at
cardboard crowns and oddments of costume from the dressing-
up box, when observation of the behaviour of children as well as
adults makes clear that the clothes and the properties of an
individual are as much an expression of his individuality as
his speech and should therefore be as intrinsic an aspect of a
child's education.

We have seen that drama draws a number of 'subjects'
together and gives opportunity for their development in a
personal and imaginative contact. This is wholly in keeping
with the methods used in many primary schools where teachers
are increasingly interested in establishing a close relationship
between the different subjects and obliterating artificial
distinctions. This gives a certain imprecision to what we mean
by drama while offering at the same time almost limitless scope.
Let us therefore look at some of the different kinds of drama
likely to be found in a junior school.

First of all we might take the drama that derives from
children's play. A teacher saw a group of boys playing cowboys

and Indians in the field outside the school. When the children came back into the classroom at the end of break he began to ask them about cowboys. They told him what they knew. He told them about the conquest of America and why the cowboys and the early explorers had come into conflict with the Indians. The group who had been playing in the field asked whether they could continue with their game. The teacher encouraged the rest of the class to join in. Some became explorers, some cowboys, some Indians, and the girls took their place in the various tribes and communities that were being created.

This particular game won the interest of the children so completely that it developed into a project on the North American continent that lasted for many weeks. The teacher sent some children to the library to find books about the Indians. They made headdresses and tepees. They studied Indian art. They learnt about the Great Prairies and the Rocky Mountains and the Pacific Ocean. They hunted buffalo and searched for gold. They wrote and drew abundantly, they made innumerable models, they acted scores of scenes. But this is not to say that every game turns out to be so productive. It is one of the greatest skills of the teacher to detect the impulse in the children that might be profitably developed, and how to do it. But every teacher must be prepared for failure. The idea may just not catch on as this one did.

Some teachers use drama to encourage children to create characters from their own imagination, to explore situations or relationships of their own contriving, and to invent their own improvized stories. Here the teacher must show the greatest skill in accepting whatever the children offer and helping them to shape the idea dramatically. It is only from experience of success and failure that we come to realize the ideas that can be expressed in drama and those that are not suitable, as we have to learn the kind of shapes that can and cannot be made out of clay and the ideas that lend themselves to expression in poetry or prose.

Drama often emerges from movement. One teacher gave children an opportunity to move to different kinds of music. She used a variety of orchestral and instrumental music and carefully noted to which pieces the children responded most readily and in what way. She then played some electronic music and asked the children to make their own sounds and move to them. This involved them happily for several lessons in creating all the spirits of the underworld—witches, goblins, gnomes, elves and varieties of creatures of no known origin. To provide a contrast she then moved to music of a more ritualistic quality. One kind of procession led to another. They searched their minds for every kind of ritual and procession and their collection of records for appropriate music. This led them finally to the procession of children at the end of the Pied Piper of Hamelin and having begun with the end they went back to the beginning and spent several weeks dramatizing the whole story with a mixture of their own words and those of Robert Browning.

Drama has traditional links with English and history. It draws much of its material from myth and legend, the Bible, epic poetry, and historical episodes. Sensitive teachers are sometimes concerned at the inaccuracies attendant on any dramatization of a specific event. Examples have already been given of incongruities of language. But the purpose of dramatization is not to present a number of accurate facts. This is the function of books and source material. The purpose of drama is to provide for a kind of personal involvement that extends the imagination beyond what is possible from pictures and narrative and other sources, thereby providing some kind of perception of what it must have been like 'to be there'. One recalls many dramatizations of the Nativity story. One group of children enjoyed a vigorous scene among guests at the inn with the three Magi, one of whom was good King Wenceslas, drinking deeply with the shepherds. A group of boys made a vivid scene of the shepherds after putting all the girls in the class on their hands and knees as sheep penned within a stockade of chairs. They were attacked by a pack of wolves, fought them off, and had just finished burying the corpses when Gabriel—excused from duty as a sheep—appeared in the night sky. One recalls with pleasure a group of 7 year olds who had heard about the Vikings from their teachers and had constructed in the midst of their classroom a boat in which they were rowing up the Thames to plunder a Saxon settlement.

The teacher had to persuade them that there would be greater benefits in carrying off treasure than Saxon maidens. A remarkable flow of language and of logical argument came from a class of top juniors who in recent years have dramatized such subjects as Saint Joan, the story of Ahab and Jezebel, and an episode from seventeenth-century history when plague in a Derbyshire village led to a vicious witch-hunt. The teacher concerned claims that he takes drama with the children to increase their powers of conceptual thought and it was astonishing to hear children, with an I.Q. that suggested near illiteracy, argue with imaginative breadth, intellectual insight, and emotional passion, always moving the story forward, but extracting every minute implication from each scene as it arose.

There are two further points which call for comment. As will have been noted, the emphasis is on improvization. Most teachers believe that a rich and varied experience of the kind of work that has been described in this chapter is necessary before children can handle a text without an embarrassing stiffness and artificiality. To create a character that is depicted only in the words he has to say in the limited situations presented in the play is an extraordinarily difficult feat and beyond the capabilities of most children of primary school age. While there is much to be said for this point of view, it should be added that the inability of many children to read or speak aloud somebody else's words convincingly is because they have very little experience of doing it. The escape from formality has brought considerable advantages to primary education but it is just as important that, in their work in English, children should hear the way in which the great poets have used language as it is that they should visit museums and picture galleries to see the way in which the masters have used clay and paint.

Other teachers are critical of the extent to which children are discouraged from appearing in front of an audience. There is nothing definitive that can be said about this. The artificiality and the self-consciousness of many dramatic performances in primary schools are something that all sensitive teachers wish to avoid. Yet there is a proper instinct in children to wish to show and to share their work. It seems therefore that the decision must lie with the teacher. She alone will know whether the work is sufficiently clear to make sense to a small audience of other children. She will also ensure that children are sufficiently secure in what they are doing to give their play without falling into artificiality on the one hand, or showing-off on the other. There is nothing wrong with performance to an audience so long as it is appreciated as an important stage of development for which children must be ready and prepared.

Many of these decisions are not difficult to make when the teacher knows why he or she is doing drama with the children. A London teacher attempted a definition in the following terms:

It is a form of creative expression. Since basically it involves no more than being able to move and speak, it is accessible to everyone. From the self-centred and instinctive dramatic play of young children it develops into a unique form of creative contact between individuals. Many natural resources, personal abilities, and acquired skills can be used constructively and at the same time. Thus drama can claim to make a contribution to the full education of a human being.

We might do worse than this.

FOR FURTHER READING

Education Survey No. 2—Drama, H.M.S.O., 1968.
Way, Brian, *Development Through Drama*, Longmans, 1967.
Hodgson, J., and Richards, E., *Improvisation*, Methuen, 1966.

9. Movement

Ruth Foster

IT IS often said that 'Children are the same all the world over'; if this were true then it seems likely that we could quite properly provide similar opportunities for them all the world over. But is the young child who has been carried on his mother's back and, presumably, intimately involved in the rhythm of her movement, the same as one who has been pushed in a pram and who has learnt as soon as possible to sit up for his meals at a table while in another country he might have squatted on the floor?

The musical rhythms enjoyed by, for example, African, West Indian or Eastern children seem incomprehensibly complex to a child brought up in the musical traditions of the West; in some communities dancing and music are part of everyday life, and the children pick up for themselves the pattern and mode of music and movement; in others—dancing may be relegated entirely to special places and occasions, it may be regarded as effeminate and something that needs to be taught.

The local or national heroes may be athletes, cricketers, rugger or soccer players, tennis players or dancers, and the impact of their image on the young of that nation or community (village, town or school) is often very strong, and influences the 'natural' behaviour of children quite as much as any formal programme that is prepared for them by adults.

In one family the children may appear sedate and tidy, in another in the same community, careless and uproarious. Even within the same family there is great variety—exuberant children in sedate families, quiet ones among the uproarious, boys who prefer fishing to football, and girls who would as soon sail a boat or ride a pony as play with dolls, and sit in a tree as readily as on a chair.

The pattern and pressures of the community, the prestige of the heroes (masculine and feminine) are very strong. How far then can it be true that 'Children are the same all the world over'? Is it possible that, despite community pressures and practices, there are certain innate characteristics in which children everywhere are nearer to each other than they are to adults in their own community?

Rabindranath Tagore is reported as saying 'My grand-child tries to speak to me with her whole body'* and this total involvement of feeling, sound, word and action in communication must be familiar to every mother from the moment of her baby's first cry and kick, right through the period when actions and sounds become more specific, when words and locomotion on all fours are superseded by the revelation of the world that comes from achieving the upright position and single words develop into the growth of language. Through all these phases, movement, mood and words are part of the same process of learning and expressing. There are some communities in which Tagore's grandchild would find herself at home even as an adult, though in a more restrained mode perhaps.

Another characteristic of children everywhere is mobility in movement enabling them to perform impossible (that is un-predictable) feats and opening up for them a whole field of exploration and invention. It is a characteristic that is dimin-ished early in an urban environment where children sit at tables, travel in cars, buses and trains. Physiologically, children 'burn up' more rapidly than adults and this, together with their anatomical mobility, tends to make them lively, restless, ex-ploratory, resilient, spontaneous and, often, noisy. Mysteriously, children of different races seem to us not to have much difficulty in understanding each other's language; there seems to be a common currency in action—sound—speech. The *quality* of the complex–action/speech—seems to convey understanding at a stage when words do not mean one thing and action another.

We may describe three main aspects of a child's development in and through movement: (1) his skill, (2) his exploration of

* 'Rabindranath Tagore, Pioneer in Education", essays and exchanges between Rabindranath Tagore and L. K. Elmhirst.

the environment, (3) his expressive powers. These are not separate but related and, indeed, overlapping categories.

1. *Skill*. Whether it is a child's first few steps, his ability to throw and (more difficult) to catch a ball, to jump over an obstacle, climb a tree, swim across a stream, ride a bicycle, stand on his head or turn a cartwheel, there is always great pleasure in the sheer sensation of the experience and in the achievement itself rather than in its usefulness. There is also a powerful impact on the child's image of himself. While this image (or idea of himself) is built up in all sorts of ways (for example, by other people's comments on him) experiences in which movement plays a main part are especially powerful. When for the first time he stands up-right alone, his view of the world, and of himself in that world, must change dramatically. To climb up a tree changes him again, and so does flying along on a bicycle or standing on his head.

2. *Exploration of the Environment*. Probably in the first place it is through touch and reach that a baby begins to explore and recognize his environment. Then, as powers of locomotion develop, he begins to build up concepts of space—distances, heights and, through increasingly discriminating powers of touch and grasp and greater strength, he understands more and more of the nature of things. We begin to understand space when we traverse it, weight when we handle it, and time in relation to both. We tend to forget the interaction between visual and kinaesthetic experience, yet a spire appears to 'soar', arches 'spring', vistas 'stretch', domes 'swell', roads 'climb' hills and paths 'wind' through woods. These uses of language illustrate something of the nature of our experience in the field of movement (qualitative as well as quantitative) and its contribution to visual perception.

3. *Expressive Powers*. In every action there is an expressive element. For example, we recognize a friend at a distance by his mode of walking before we can see his face clearly,

and we may well judge his mood by a noticeable quality in his walk or his gestures. But in many activities the expressive element is incidental. It is when emotion is deeply stirred and communication is important that the expressive element dominates. In children this element is not subdued and cut off from other kinds of action as it tends to be in Western adults. Sheer agility may quickly light up into exuberant leaping and prancing, which becomes dancelike, or a dance may embody elements of shouting, singing and stamping which are near to music. A large and important chair may be something to climb on and jump off, but it may also trigger off a way of sitting down in which the rôle played is that of an important person. Children often dance, or move in a dancelike way when they are excited or, as we say, above themselves. If they do not, the excitement may end in temper and aggression.

If children are to live abundantly their experiences in movement are clearly of great importance. What opportunities do they need?

One of the hardest things for any teacher to decide is the terms of reference within which he will work. What time? Which space? What equipment? This story or that story? This music or that or none? What degree of freedom? What specific instruction? When? Perhaps the best general guidance in trying to answer these questions is to observe, understand and be guided by the nature of the children's play.

Ideally, opportunities should differ in kind according to the general pattern of living. For example, in some urban schools with crowded classrooms in which children sit at desks most of the day, a period of movement can do little more than serve as a very necessary release and it will not be easy for the children to become deeply involved and to develop varied resources. Where the pattern of the day is much more natural, with children moving freely about the classroom, the time devoted specifically to movement need not merely serve as a relief but can also be devoted to a richer development of the children's natural powers.

Children need space (this in itself may trigger off invention) and time. Some of the space needs to be open to permit running, leaping, chasing and playing with balls, and some needs to be more diverse so that climbing, rolling, creeping, swinging and jumping in all sorts of ways can be enjoyed. In some climates a large space indoors is also necessary, not only to provide shelter but also the clean surface and the contained environment that some aspects of movement need.

A pool (even a small one) helps the children's delight in play in water to develop easily into the skill of swimming.

It has been suggested that children, partly because of their anatomical and physiological make-up, are exploratory and inventive and it seems very important that this stage of their lives should be enjoyed to the full. At the same time the development of skills needs practice, practice that children will often pursue for themselves, and the adult has, somehow to balance the opportunities for exploration with those for repetition. It is tempting for the adult to decide much too narrowly the kind of skill to be developed, and to think in stereotyped terms. In England we may have learnt something of the versatility of children through the introduction into primary schools of climbing equipment of a kind that no adult had ever used before and which led children to find out for themselves what they could do. What happened went so far beyond our imaginings that it has had an impact on the opportunities we have provided in other directions, though the pressures on boys to be taught set techniques in games and athletics at an early age remain considerable.

It is clear that the kind of opportunities that may be given in the specific time devoted to movement will extend children's understanding of space (vertical as well as horizontal) and weight, and, through touch, of quality. But this growth of perception extends, slowly or quickly, narrowly or broadly, to all activity, whether at home or in school. It is only necessary here to suggest that understanding of the place of movement in this connection is important and that the environment, including materials for building and making, should be rich and varied.

In England we tend to think of two categories of expressive experience in which movement is a main factor—dance and drama. But children do not behave like this and express their ideas and feelings in a mixture of ways, and in some countries even adults use one word for music—dance—drama.

Again, in this field, there is the problem of deciding when to leave children free to discover and create without intervention, and when to help them more specifically to develop resources that will help to carry them further. Where emotion is a powerful force the need is not to *re*press but to help children to *ex*press, that is not to explode, or describe, but to give shape and form to that which stirs them deeply. 'The importance for the child of finding ordered release for the emotions, in sport or in arts, would seem to be the natural door to release through the mind and the wits, and so to the right path to thought and to intellectual activity. But to love, the ultimate aim, the start must be emotional expression in as many directions as possible or available and gradually to achieve an ordered expression.'*

Adults often forget that for children, movement, quite as much as words, is a vital and most immediate means of expression and that in the expressive aspect of their living their whole being is very deeply involved.

Are children the same all the world over? In that they differ in make-up and modes of movement from the adults of their own race, and in these respects resemble and understand each other more closely, the answer is probably 'yes'.

FOR FURTHER READING

Tagore, R. and Elmhirst, L. K., *Rabindranath Tagore, Pioneer in Education*, Murray, 1961.
Moving and Growing, H.M.S.O., 1958.
Drama—Education Survey 2, H.M.S.O., 1968.
Story of a School, H.M.S.O., 1958.
Jordan, D., *Childhood and Movement*, Blackwell, 1960.

* Dr L. K. Elmhirst, op. cit.

10. Art

Sybil Marshall

THE GREAT changes that have overtaken the primary schools of England in the last twenty-five years began, to a very large extent, in the field of art. In the 1930s art suddenly became 'free' in every sense of the word. In doing so, it pointed the way to freedom for the rest of the curriculum.

Until that time, the word 'art' had not been applied to what children did in the primary school. The rigid timetables of the first quarter of the century indicated that 'Drawing' took place once or twice a week. What actually went on in those 'drawing' lessons was very much of the same nature as what went on in all other lessons—English, arithmetic, history, or anything else. The lesson consisted of a teacher doggedly trying to make children accept adult concepts and adult standards, and to use adult techniques and skills long before they had even come to terms with infant ones. The poor children were not being asked to run before they could walk—they were being commanded to fly. The result, of course, was bewilderment, failure and fear on the part of the pupils, and resigned frustration on the part of the teacher. In those days, many an intelligent teacher must have asked himself what purpose it all served: if he had been bold enough to ask the question out loud, he would have been told that drawing provided a useful exercise in 'discipline' and gave the children a chance to learn manual control.

In fact, the methods of those days completely ignored the children in their own right as living, thinking, feeling human beings. It simply wasted their precious 'growing time'—worse, indeed, for the endless, hopeless attempts at drawing some such object as teacher's chair, or occasionally the meticulous copying of a spray of leaves, set up in the majority of the child-

120

ren feelings of utter ineptitude, combined with resentment and
rebellion against the authority that persistently demanded
from them such nonsensical irrelevance. Secondly, this boring
'learning to draw' ignored art in its own right as the means by
which the human spirit discovers itself, encourages itself,
enlarges itself and purifies itself. (Art in this context includes
all the arts, of course.)

Then, suddenly, common sense broke through, largely due
to the efforts of Marion Richardson and her disciples who tried
out in all schools, even the very academic grammar schools of
the day, the theories progressive educationists had previously
been promulgating for the infant schools. The basis of the new
approach was that a child exists, feels and acts as a child.
When he meets a new experience, he wants to use it, to make
it his own, to do something with it in a childlike way. One of
these ways is to depict the experience in some medium or
other. What experiences he will choose to depict, out of the
many that come his way every hour that he lives, cannot be
forecast. That is his own concern. However, in order to be able
to satisfy himself when he chooses to depict any experience,
he must be in control of the tools he is using, whatever they
may be. The tools must therefore be suited to the size of his
hands and the state of his muscular control. In addition, as a
child reacts to colour instinctively, it is reasonable to suppose
that to work in a colour medium instead of black-and-white
will have more direct appeal to him.

As soon as the Second World War was over and materials
became available again, these new ideas began to spread.
Children everywhere began to find delight and release of
imaginative power in the freedom of the 'art period' (no longer
the 'drawing lesson'!). Large sheets of cheap paper, large, fat
brushes of hog-bristle, and containers of bright pigment in
powder form which mixed at a touch with water replaced the
hard pencils and expensive cartridge paper 'drawing-books' of
pre-war days. There was no longer a command to 'draw' a
certain object chosen by the teacher; instead, there was an
open invitation to symbolize in picture form some experience
of their own. The revolution had begun, but it was by no means
over, for no one in those early days could have foretold the

explosion of freedom from the shackles of past educational practice this breakthrough in the field of art heralded.

In the first place, the work the children produced under the new conditions gave teachers everywhere a great deal to think about. Working with materials they enjoyed, in an atmosphere of relaxing freedom, the children were prolific to an extent that would previously have been considered impossible. Even more startling was the quality of what they produced in such enormous quantity. While not measuring up to those standards of adult representational art that had so far been the criterion, they nevertheless set new standards of their own, throwing new light on the workings of the child's imagination, and giving an entire new range of aesthetic values until then unsuspected and unappreciated. To put it simply, we found that in our adult pride and ignorance we had constantly *underestimated the ability of children*, and because we, the ignorant adults, were in authority, we had actually been holding back their burgeoning ability to learn and to achieve. Moreover, it was soon revealed, contrary to any belief held in the past, that the instinct of children is towards what is aesthetically of high quality. Their basic taste is *good*. Yet for many decades at least, a fifth-rate standard of conformity had been pressed upon them, to the complete exclusion and repression of anything that arose naturally from 'the shaping spirit of their imagination'.

These revelations had far-reaching effects. The children were teaching their educators how to use paint. It was not long before it dawned on the brightest of those educators that what applied to paint probably applied to other things. A few bold spirits introduced into their classrooms other media by which pictures could be made—things like fat wax crayons, pastels, and coloured inks. Others, alarmed at the cost of keeping enthusiastic classes of more than forty little artists supplied with a constant flow of expensive paint, looked around for less expensive media with which to improvize. This was perhaps one of the most significant developments, for it meant that for the first time the teacher had been forced into a situation in which he, too, had to use his imaginative faculties. One of the solutions found was the 'paper mosaic', a method in which colour is supplied by cutting up and sticking on to a sketched background the coloured illustrations of cheap, weekly magazines and journals. The only materials required for this were a pile of old magazines, a pair of scissors (and even the scissors could be dispensed with if necessary, small fingers being adept at tearing), and a pot of some reasonably clean adhesive. Again, once this idea had been thoroughly explored, there were lateral developments. 'Mosaics' are built up of small irregular pieces of glass, or stones, or tiny tiles set into a material, plastic while wet but hard when dry. Imitation mosaics could be built up with materials that could be obtained merely for the trouble of collecting them, particularly natural things like straw, for instance. They could be used in their natural colour, or stained with dye or ink, seeds of all kinds, like those of the sunflower or vegetable marrow, being ideal. Nowadays, there are specially prepared adhesives that will hold even weighty objects like stones and shells securely in place on a background of paper; in the early days of experiment with such things in schools, these wonderful adhesives were simply not available, and substitutes had to be found. The obvious base for mosaics was clay, not the expensive refined potter's clay now common in schools as a medium for pottery and sculpture, but common clay dug direct from the school garden. The disadvantages of this were obvious, the main one being that it dried too quickly and as soon as it did, it cracked, and the art-work just fell to pieces. Did that really matter? Would it matter now? Surely not, for the object of art in schools is not to produce durable works, but to exercise the imaginative spirit of the human child. (It is worth remarking, in passing, that in the Midlands of England, particularly in Derbyshire, there exists an age-old custom of 'dressing the wells' in certain villages. This is done by erecting over the well-head a picture, sometimes of dimensions as large as eight feet by five feet, made up entirely of flower petals and other natural materials like cotton grass and onion skins embedded in clay. The clay is kept moist by the application of water at regular intervals, and these marvellous works of art have, in this way, a life of approximately one week's duration. Their evanescence is part of their charm. That they are worth the effort involved, no one doubts, especially the artists themselves, that is, the men and women of the villages who have handed down this beautiful art from father to son and from mother to daughter, for centuries, probably back to pagan times. And what an extraordinary reflection it is upon 'education' that the children of Derbyshire at the beginning of this century knew how to execute an art form as delightful and unusual as this, while sitting bored and fearful at their desks in the village school attempting to draw teacher's tea-pot or walking-stick with a hard pencil on unsuitable paper!)

'Sticking things on' became a further development, that before long became known to schools, as it is elsewhere in the world of art, as 'collage'.

The basic material used in collage in most English schools is fabric—scraps of dress and furnishing textiles, collected by the children (and teachers) and enhanced and supplemented by such oddments as beads, buttons, sequins, trimmings of lace, braid and ribbon, fur and feathers. But once the idea has taken root, the number of things that can be used for this sort of picture-making is legion—straw and grass, dried leaves, seeds and seedcases; stones, shells, bark and twigs; string and thread, especially such as will easily unravel, wool and cotton; and even more unexpected things like fish-bones (dried and cleaned, of course), iron filings, and a variety of industrial waste materials. What all this really adds up to is that the children are being invited to experiment *in the creative use of whatever materials lie ready to hand*. Most schools do, in fact, still rely heavily on paint and crayon, used on a reasonably tough 'sugar' paper; but the more progressive ones add an infinite variety of materials to their pupils' experience by mosaic and collage, in both cases making as much use of natural and cheap materials from the immediate environment as possible. In the list of such truly progressive schools must be counted the many, small, rural schools whose budgets do not allow them to purchase lavishly art supplies produced commercially, but who nevertheless practise real education through art by improvizing imaginatively with the aid of waste and junk material.

Once picture-making has been extended to include collage, it lies very close to the three-dimensional world of craft. Take the question of 'needlework', for example. It would obviously be easy to draw a parallel between the changes in art and those in needlework, from the days of the tear-and-blood-stained hem of a duster to the gorgeous riot of imaginative work produced with fabric and thread today. The significant thing, however, is not that, but the fact that thirty years ago 'needlework' and 'drawing' bore no relationship whatsoever to each other except for the fact that girls often did the former while boys did the latter. Today they are twins, born of the same creative impulses, fed by the same imaginative response to materials, and mutually dependent. The knowledge of the nature of fabrics and textiles acquired while using them for making pictures is a pre-requisite for true needlecraft: no less so the cutting and shaping, the colour matching and the familiarity with the intricacies of overall patterns and designs. In return, the skilled use of the needle for applying one material to another, for attaching things together and for inventing intricate patterns in fine threads gives generously to the understanding of design and to achievement in art work in general.

The cutting and sticking of materials lead the way also to other crafts like taking rubbings, and the many techniques of low-relief work, such as modelling in papier mâché, balsawood or expanded polystyrene, and in casting in sand and clay.

All this must make it plain that one of the results of the revolution in art teaching has been the closing of the gap between the so-called 'subjects' in the curriculum. This may be a direct consequence of the discovery that it is not necessary to separate from each other the various media used in the course of straight-forward picture-making. The multiplicity of effect one can obtain by mixing media has truly to be tried to be believed—paint with wax-crayon, with pencil, chalk, charcoal, ink, or any permutation of these: mosaic and collage combined, with paint or crayon to fill in the background, and black ink to add the finer details: needle and thread always at hand to add pattern or decoration, even on the flimsiest of paper backgrounds—these are but a few of the ways that have served to show that 'creative' art is a reality in more ways than one. (It is worth noting that a flowering in craft almost equal to that in art has also shown itself lately in our schools, in claywork (pottery and sculpture), bookcrafts, modelling in all sorts of materials, and puppetry, to name but a few crafts to be seen in the majority of primary schools.)

The new type adhesives have made three-dimensional work easy as well as popular, and in infant schools the concept of 'art' includes such activities as modelling with 'junk', making houses, castles, fairy palaces or Dyak long houses, large enough to get into for play purposes, from cardboard boxes and grocery cartons, and the designing and making up of clothes for proper dramatic play.

Before leaving the subject of creative work for its own sake, and for the sake of nurturing to the full the creative impulse which every child in some measure appears to possess, we ought briefly to discuss the sort of things children choose to depict in their artwork, and the rôle the teacher plays in helping his pupils to progress.

One could almost make a bald statement that there is nothing children will not attempt, once they have learned enough control of their materials to taste achievement and success. It is, however, possible to make three broad divisions in what they do, and why they do it. There are those processes chosen simply because the children love the doing of them. Cutting and sticking come into this category, and so do rubbing and taking impressions in clay. The results of their efforts may not be pictures or patterns in the strict sense of these terms. There is a danger here for the teacher. Obviously, children doing these things for the sake of doing them are learning while experimenting, and such joyful experimentation must be encouraged, *but recognized for what it is.* If the children set out to 'make a pattern' by any of these means, well and good, so long as they possess the basic understanding that patterns are meant to be used, usually in the decoration of some other object such as a page of a book, or a pot, or a piece of fabric. There are still too many schools in which 'making patterns' in paint or crayon, paper or 'collage from oddments' is a time-filler which never gets anywhere in its own right, but does become an obstacle to progress in picture-making. Worse still is the acceptance, day after day, by many teachers, of a panel composed of a conglomeration of disparate materials stuck haphazardly together, as 'abstract work'. To the small child, the interest in such a piece of 'work' has been in the sticking, and as such the work is valid. For the teacher to pretend it is *art*, by any standards other than his own purely subjective ones, is dangerous nonsense. Children are no more able to deal with abstract concepts in art than they are in mathematics or grammar.

Then again, children will celebrate or 'symbolize' experience of a significant kind to them, personally, in pictures. As these pictures arise in every case from individual experience, it is always difficult for the teacher to assess their value altogether as art. They may, and often do, have considerable merit as art. in which case there is no difficulty. But they may be repetitious attempts by the child to come to terms with some sort of experience, sad experiences such as death, loss, fear, hate, rejection, failure, anger—or conversely the equally repetitious desire to recapture delight or pleasure, even such an 'everyday' pleasure as watching the garage hand fill the tank of a passing car from a petrol pump. As it is the function of the teacher to see that the child progresses, he must be aware when a child becomes 'stuck in a groove' of this kind, apparently unable to extricate himself. If it is plain to the teacher that the child is actually using art, especially as a therapeutic agent, it is well to leave well alone; but if it becomes obvious that he is merely making the same statements again and again without using any imagination it is time for the teacher to exercise some coercion in order to get him to move on.

The third category of what children will do covers most of the true art done in schools. It includes both the other categories, but uses the children's innate good taste, their growing skill and technical ability, and their desire to achieve by creating works that can be enjoyed by others. Teachers have come to regard themselves as promoters of situations that will introduce experiences of a new and stimulating kind. This includes sensory experience and the experience of imagination as well. They take care, therefore, to promote situations which can be explored in as many ways as possible, in language, movement, drama, sound, art and craft. They help the children to select which art will best symbolize which experience, make practical suggestions with regard to choice of materials, and give help and advice when things go wrong. When art is produced in this way, it is truly educational, for the whole set-up is an ideal one from an educational standpoint, the willing child working under the supervision of an interested adult trained to advise and appreciate, but not to interfere.

The new approach to art was not long in spilling over into other subjects, particularly English, where the same experiments in child-freedom met with the same encouraging results. More recently, it has been tried out in the field of music. Gone, with the drawing of the school bell and the everlasting composition about 'What I did at the Weekend', are the days when children stood in straight lines droning national songs or lugubrious hymns. Instead, they experiment with percussion and melody-making instruments (many of them home-made) creating music as they create pictures or drama.

This broadening of the scope of each subject to the point at which it overlaps other subjects has given rise to a new concept of what the curriculum in its entirety is. As more and more of the divisions between the subjects become blurred and indistinct in practice, progressive educators realize that those divisions, admitted and acted upon though they were for so long, were, in fact, unreal. Experience, the substance of the curriculum, is whole and undivided, though it may be looked at from many different angles, and explored from many different starting points.

Art was one of the first subjects to be correlated deliberately with others. The days of mere 'correlation' are, however, now giving way fast to complete 'integration' of the entire curriculum and of the time at the child's disposal in school. In such conditions, what is the rôle of art in a truly progressive primary school using an integrated curriculum and an integrated time schedule?

First, it exists in its own right as an activity which develops the child's powers of expression with regard to his environment, and as a partner to craft.

Next, it exists as one of several means for the symbolization of experience. Let us suppose the children have spent an afternoon exploring the nearest park, or wood, or seashore, or riverbank, or canal, or farmyard, or building site—or anything else; in the days following, this experience will be assessed, re-lived, re-explored and re-enjoyed in imagination as the children gradually assimilate it, in the same way that food is used when it is ingested. Art will be one of the ways in which it will be used. They may paint straightforward pictures of the expedition as a whole, or select tiny aspects of which they only were conscious, and blow these small things up to large size. They may make imaginative leaps away from the the central experience, in which the wood becomes a jungle, the municipal car-park a space-station, the council house under erection a medieval castle, the pet-shop a Noah's Ark. They will employ any technique they choose to portray their idea, and maybe, while out, collect materials for it on the spot. They will also record their trip in language, illustrating their stories as they go along, this time using neater, smaller ways of producing pictorial art; for the days when art always meant fat brushes and powder tempera are, in their turn, at an end. Children can create art using any materials and any tools.

The class may decide to make a co-operative record of their visit, either in book form or by making a large frieze for the classroom wall. If the former, it will be illustrated with individual pictures in any known technique. If the latter, it may be an enormous collage in which the children work together using materials gathered on the site to splendid advantage.

Stories, poems, songs and music all become springboards from which expression in the form of pictorial art can take flight. History and geography, while no longer appearing on the timetable as isolated subjects, are given scope as aspects of any experience, and demand expression and investigation in and through art. Religious education, still compulsory, is both helped and inspired by art, in the same way as religion has always given inspiration to the artist throughout the ages.

Lastly, there remain those aspects of experience covered by mathematics and science. For a long time, these were left outside the circle in which art was a central influence, but this is so no longer. We know now, as never before, that art and mathematics are inseparable, linked by so many strands that it is difficult to pick out one to serve as an example. To take the link at a very simple yet significant level, let us remember that the composition of any picture is an exercise in spatial relationships in which recognition of basic shapes and complete understanding of relative sizes are counters. Taking the concept of symmetry as another example, one crosses another vague and indistinct borderline into the field of science, for the world of natural history supplies examples of symmetry at every turn. In other areas of scientific exploration, pattern and colour, the pillars of art, play no small part. But for the scientist as well as the mathematician, for the poet as well as the sociologist, for the doctor and the archaeologist and the teacher, for any human being caught up in the intricacies of ordinary everyday life, early education must provide the eye that sees, the mind that comprehends, and the spirit which leaps to respond. Art teaches and develops them all. That is the real justification for the important place it has in education here today. It is, as all education everywhere should be, preparation for a happy and satisfying life as an adult, for it engenders in the human spirit an interest in those few things over which economic success or failures can have little, if any, control.

FOR FURTHER READING

Read, H., *Education Through Art*, Faber, 3rd Edition, 1958.
Jameson, K., *Pre-school and Infant Art*, Evans, 1968.
Melzi, K., *Art in The Primary School*, Chatto and Windus, 1967.
Sproule, A., *With a free hand*, Reinholf Book Corp., 1968.
Marshall, S., *Experiment in Education*, C.U.P., 1963.
Marshall, S., *Aspects of Art Work 5–9*, Evans, 1967.

11. Inside the Classroom

E. Bay Tidy

PROBABLY ONE should not take the heading of this chapter too literally, as often in modern primary schools more seems to be happening outside than inside the classroom. In fact, as one enters the school gate one is likely to see a couple of children measuring with a trundle wheel* in the playground, half a dozen more collecting leaves from the trees in order to make leaf-prints for their nature book and, on entering the school, three or four others making a large model of a space ship in the cloakroom, while just inside the classroom door four or five may be reading in a well-stocked book corner. Inside the classroom various groups or individuals will be painting, writing in diaries, making a frieze or working at a 'Discovery Table' following directions from a wall book made and illustrated by the teacher.

Classroom organization will depend partly on the way in which the school as a whole is planned. Primary schools in this country show every possible type of school organization and a corresponding variety of approaches to classroom work. Many schools are still following a very traditional programme with set syllabuses in definite subject fields, one teacher being responsible for one class all day, with the usual pattern of thirty-minute lessons, often in quite unrelated work. At the other end of the scale there are schools working with a free timetable, organized on an 'Integrated Day' basis, where one sees practically no class teaching, and where children and teachers follow individual and group activities throughout the day. In other words, classrooms vary from those in which the accent is on what the teacher can *tell* the child to those in which all kinds of activities are arranged so that children *learn*

* Trundle wheel—see Taskmaster's catalogue, Leicester LE2 3AL.

131

from materials and situations provided by the teacher. Most teachers of 5 to 7 year old children now follow the informal pattern, and those who teach the 8 to 11 year olds are, in many cases, following suit. Junior schools are slower to change as they are still somewhat overshadowed by the subject-based secondary schools and because the rich background of materials and free methods of the infant schools take much time and experimentation to make effective. However, as we have read, various Nuffield and Schools Council curriculum projects are producing materials to meet the more complex demands of the children in junior schools and in classrooms where these materials are being used there is a tendency to move from class teaching to small-group and individual work. This tendency is probably one of the strongest trends in the primary classroom today and is, in some measure, the result of the excellent experimental work done in many of our village schools.

The two-teacher village school is one of the most exciting areas of education today. Here the headteacher is usually in charge of the class of thirty to thirty-five 8 to 11 year olds, while his (or her) assistant will have the 5 to 7 year olds in another room. The accommodation may vary from the new open-plan village school of the kind built in Leicestershire, to the old church schools in Sussex that have been left with their Gothic exteriors and rebuilt in modern style behind this facade. In this type of school what is known as Vertical Grouping is forced upon the teacher as all the children of the age-range have to be in the same class. One has to 'teach' the 5 and 7 year olds together, and the 8 and 11 year olds together. It is, of course, impossible to stream the children and all intelligence ranges have to be catered for in the same class. Under these conditions class-teaching as such is virtually an impossibility, so that village schools have experimented with all kinds of group and individual work and are very much concerned with the provision of self-instructional materials which allow the children to work by themselves to a very flexible timetable.

This obviously permits good use to be made of the teacher's time. The children use the materials throughout the day and go to the teacher for set work at different times. There are, however, two conditions that must be satisfied if this system is to succeed—the material, or experience, provided for the children has to be absorbing enough to keep them involved either without the teacher or with very little help, and the teacher must set the pattern of work, perhaps for the day, perhaps for the week, depending upon the age of the children, and must ensure that it is done. In most village schools the pattern of the day is worked out so that children choose their own activities at any time of the day; the requirement that the teacher makes of them is that they must complete a certain amount of work, especially in mathematics and English, during a set time.

The day probably begins with a very short assembly taken by a group of children. One day the 10 and 11 year old children will take this, choose their own hymns, perhaps provide a soloist on the guitar, read the poems they have composed during the week, and then close with a prayer that they have probably written for themselves. On another morning the 5 and 6 year olds may run the assembly with the help of their teacher. They may show the paintings they have made the day before. The theme could be 'Colour in Spring' and they would make their contribution by telling the rest of the school about the colours in their paintings. A hymn will follow and perhaps an announcement by the teacher. This really gives a quiet period at the beginning of the day before the children begin their various activities. After this, in the junior classroom, the teacher will probably gather together the whole group of 8 to 11 year olds and tell them how much time he expects them to spend on certain tasks during the week. Usually these will include assignments in mathematics and English based on work with apparatus, on a set book, or with work cards. Some of the modern mathematics and English books are almost self-explanatory to children, and are planned for individual work and minimum teacher-help. Bell's twelve little books* (Pattern, Binary System, Sounds, etc.) and Sealey's 'Exploring Language' series† are exciting and lead individuals to exploration and discovery. Progress checkpoints are built into Sealey's book and answers to the multiple-choice questions

* *Mathematics in the Making*, Stuart Bell, Longmans, 1968.
† *Exploring Language*, Leonard Sealey, Nelson, 1968.

are provided, together with a progress chart which the child
can copy for recording his results. A contribution to a child's
individual 'Topic Book' may have to be given in at a certain
time, and groups of children will join the teacher for a poetry
session in the book-corner during the week. This means that at
any moment one can find children busily engaged upon various
parts of the curriculum. Quite often something in the environment will start off a project, or form a focal point for the
children's work. A swarm of bees in the school playground
could, for example, result in individuals or groups following this
event up, according to their age, ability and interest. The field
would be open for work in natural history, mathematics, art
and craft, creative writing, and in presenting the material
gathered in a way in which it would be available for the rest
of the class, or school, either in picture or magazine form, on
tape, or photographed and displayed as an exhibition, perhaps
for parents to see.

Many village schools become 'community schools' in which
parents play an increasing part. In one Somerset school in
which the children were following a modern mathematics
series on television, the headmaster asked parents to come to
school in groups to view these programmes with the children.
This was indeed quite a happy thought, because the mothers
came six at a time, were entertained to coffee by the staff,
viewed the programme and then were asked to help groups of
children with the work that followed the broadcast. Needless
to say, the parents were very interested in the mathematics,
which was completely new to them, and they came to understand more about the teachers' problems. This particular
school had also carried out a term's work on its own village
and, apart from the continuous work in mathematics and
English which each child had to pursue, the rest of the time
was spent in exploring the history, geography and lore of the
village. Parents were asked to turn out their attics; corn dollies,
grocery invoices and rag-books from fifty-odd years ago were
produced, as well as photographs of pinafored children dancing
round the maypole. Interviews with 'older citizens' were tape-
recorded and provided material for individual 'Topic' books
such as one on '50 Years Ago on our Farm', accompanied by

models showing the development of farm implements, and another 'Our Village Shop in Great-Grandma's Day' with a comparison of price lists. At the end of the term the school was full of exhibits of the children's work based on this particular project and presented in a great variety of ways. The Plowden Report* recognizes the importance of the part played by the village schools in establishing trends in primary education, and in using the environment, not the least important implication of which is this very interesting development in parent/teacher co-operation.

The general movement away from 'streaming' in our primary schools has meant that teachers have considered putting two or more age groups together, even in a large school. As soon as one does this it is impossible to regard the *class* as the teaching unit, and many of the schools experimenting in the field of Vertical Grouping concentrate on the group or individual. This usually means that class lessons, as such, fade out of the picture. Individual and group teaching take their place, and perhaps lead to children choosing their own work for, say, the week and taking their own time in accomplishing what the teacher has set as specific tasks. In one school, at 10 a.m. on a Friday, I found a bright 11 year old boy playing with, and understanding the principles underlying, a mathematical puzzle, 'Think-a-Dot'. He told me, with great pleasure, that he had finished his set tasks for the week and was free to 'play maths' for the rest of the day. He pointed out the teacher's weekly guidance charts which showed 'imperatives and electives'—things the children *had* to do and things they could *choose* to do. His week's tasks included an hour's individual work a day at his stage in a Programmed Maths† series (Decimal currency—pounds and pence), an hour a day on his individual topic book ('Time, and the History of Clocks') written, illustrated and accompanied by models, one hour a week's science, working with another boy on a 'Shells'‡ kit

* 'Plowden Report', *Children in Their Primary Schools*, 1967.

† Decimal Series for Primary Schools in Programmed Form (12 booklets), Foulsham Educational, Buckinghamshire, 1968.

‡ *Things of Science*. Experimental Kits for Young Children (Shells, Soil-less Garden, etc.). Things of Science, (Cambridge) Ltd, 1967.

(work cards, shells, diagrams and cardboard for experiments), as well as music-making, tape-recording the play his group had made up, and writing a story and a poem for the class magazine.

Patterns of 'freedom of choice' for children vary, but we are moving even in large schools to the integrated day, in which there is a choice of activity for every child at every moment of the day. Approaching integration gradually, many teachers, in the first instance, free just one regular period. Schools have 'Hobbies Clubs' where teachers offer their own particular interest on one afternoon a week, and the children are free to join which club they wish. Other teachers find it easier to free perhaps the art and crafts period, giving children absolute choice within just that particular part of the curriculum. Often the movement away from separate subjects is marked by a period of some integration; for example, the adoption of environmental studies which embody history, geography, English, art and crafts, and usually some science. This move is towards a more child-centred classroom in that children's interests often form the point that starts off an integrated study which cuts across all timetable and subject barriers. One such piece of thematic learning took place when ninety-six third and fourth year children and five teachers from a large South East London school spent a fortnight at the Inner London Education Authority's rural centre. They made a study of the immediate environment and undertook a planned programme of educational visits. When the party returned, three of the teachers joined together and took these children as a corporate group one-and-a-half days a week for follow-up work. The diagram on p. 138 shows the interests that the children chose to pursue during these 'free' days. As the work proceeded the three members of staff found it necessary to locate types of work such as modelling, painting, quiet investigation from books and other activities in each of the three classrooms. They also decided to specialize in one of the three sides of the work themselves. This prevented confusion and sorted the children out so that they could go to the member of staff concerned with the particular activity they had in hand. For example, Mr X dealt with all the large-scale modelling, Miss Y helped the children write their booklets and showed them how to find out facts and figures from books. The following diagram gives some idea of the range of work.

Corridors and lobbies were used to give the children as much space as possible in which to work. All the doors of the class-rooms were left open so that children could go freely from place to place, for materials or advice. Each child had complete freedom to pursue whatever interest he wished, but it was expected that at the end he would produce either an illustrated book of some kind, a tape-recording, a model, a painting or poem so that other children would understand what he had been doing.

*'The advantages of the blocked and flexible timetable based on this fortnight's visit seemed to be that the children were involved in a way not noticed before. There was a very busy atmosphere and the children had to use their own initiative. They learned to work in groups and to listen to and accept different points of view. They were also encouraged to be critical of their own and other people's work and so improve the standard all round. Great interest in the work was shown by other children in the school, and much of it was on show. Some really ambitious and large-scale modelling took place as the children had a long period in which to do this, and one particular member of staff was especially interested in, and adept at, this kind of work. There were, however, drawbacks; the model-makers took up a good deal too much of the staff's time, materials tended to 'disappear' because it was not being put back in the right places, some of the written work was apt to be a little careless because the children were not supervised as closely as they would have been in a formal lesson. In addition, some children finished their contributions before others and, therefore, had to be channelled into something new.' It was also 'difficult to keep a check on all the children and to make sure that some did not waste time and others did not work at a lower level than in fact they need have done'.

These are the criticisms made by staff members, and it is interesting to see how they tried to cope with the difficulties

---

* Data from Miss A. Grigg's detailed report to the Nuffield Resources for Learning Project (unpublished).

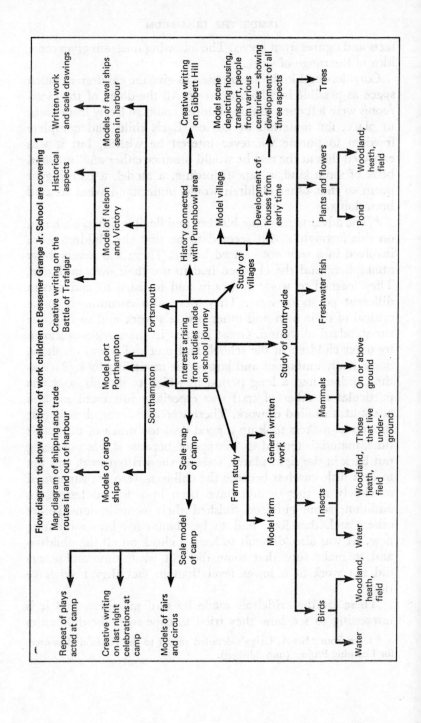

of this first large-scale project. As an extension of this project it was decided to suggest activities for the children who did not, in fact, go on the school journey, and the diagram reproduced on p. 140 was made and distributed to the staff.

The rest of the staff were, of course, consulted about this diagram and were eager that the first and second year children should join in. This they did, and on one-and-a-half days a week all staff were then available for certain aspects of the work in certain rooms and the children worked on their own interests, moving from place to place, as they wished, in order to get materials or guidance. Again, in order that every child in the school could see what had been done by the others, an exhibition took place at the end of the term.

Staff discussion at the end of this project revealed that much more staff co-operation had taken place during this work than ever before, and it was planned to do another piece of work increasing the possibilities of team, or co-operative teaching, with a large number of children engaged on a project. It was decided that the whole of the autumn term could profitably be devoted to a piece of thematic team teaching on mediaeval England, culminating in a miracle play to be performed by the whole school at Christmas.

All classes undertook to study some aspect of mediaeval life as well as to take part in the play, and each teacher (or group of teachers working together) made a sub-plan. Two teachers worked closely together on the drama and movement. Three others co-operated in training the choir, the recorder group and the orchestra; they prepared work together and followed it up by periods of critical assessment. Costumes and scenery were made by the children, staff, school-keeper and parents, the latter actually working in school during school time. Work on the theme went ahead concurrently with the normal programme of English, mathematics, physical education and games, although, as Christmas approached, the timetabling of these had to be extremely flexible in order to give groups of children a chance to meet, rehearse, or complete their work on the theme.

This interesting term's work, done by some 370 children together with twelve teachers, resulted in two performances of

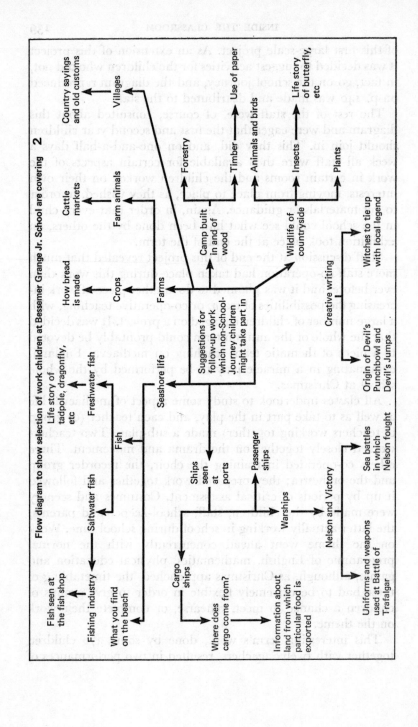

Flow diagram to show selection of work children at Bessemer Grange Jr. School are covering

a highly successful play, accompanied by an exhibition which filled the school. The area outside one classroom was taken up with a large collage—pictures and three-dimensional people—entitled 'Costumes of the Court'; part of the corridor was populated by models and big paintings of pilgrims and knights and, in an adjoining classroom, stood a large-scale model of a portcullis and drawbridge, the result of much research by children and teachers. The foyer became the castle interior, with its tapestry, suits of armour, model loom, spinning wheel, shields, banners, spears and swords, while the second half of the corridor was decorated with stained-glass windows, gargoyles and statues. In addition to this, children's booklets on their own particular piece of 'research', some of which revealed an extremely high standard of individual effort in both content and presentation, were on show. The headteacher of the school followed up this work by asking the staff to assess it after the vacation, and they were given the following questions to answer:

(a) What was the biggest advantage?
(b) What was the biggest disadvantage—
    (i)   to any individual child,
    (ii) to your class generally,
    (iii) to you personally?

The staff agreed to answer these questions in order to evaluate the work, and to try to be objective and to give independent opinions.

Their comments indicated that the main disadvantage seemed to have stemmed from the organization. To involve the whole school in a major project of this kind needed a very different type of organization from the usual class/subject compartmental pattern. The chief advantage seemed to be that many children facing difficulties within their own *class* benefited by the change to a different *group*. The children seemed to enjoy a feeling of working together; the staff gained from working in co-operation with each other, appreciated more of each other's talents and exchanged ideas much more freely. The headteacher felt that the whole school developed a definite entity which it had not done previously.

As teachers move away from the idea of teaching in a 'box', so our buildings tend to follow suit. The classrooms, instead of being boxes, have moved more and more towards an open-plan type of design and we now have a place for each activity; instead of all children working at their own desks, we find informal grouping at interest tables and in 'workshop' corners. Moving towards an even more flexible timetable, the school (or room) is arranged in bays differentiated as work areas such as art and crafts, mathematics, music and reading, so that children may choose a suitable place of work. The furniture in this type of integrated-day, open-plan school is usually used as a means of separating bays. The buildings themselves have gone through many changes and some of our most recent open-plan schools, which have no classrooms at all, are proving extremely interesting to work in. Here the spaces, the corridors, the open alcoves and the halls are designated as work areas. At one of the best known open-plan schools in London* there are no classrooms as such. Each space opens into another space and the children are regulated by their needs to use the work areas. One school in Oxfordshire† has two, large, open spaces, each housing four teachers, joined by a central hall and large circulating space. The four corners of each area are used by the teachers as a 'home' area for their 'home' group, and are carpeted so that children can sit on the floor to listen to a story or instructions. The rest of the space is planned as work areas. The teachers making up this team of four have their own particular skills and are responsible for work in one of the work areas, e.g. art and crafts. Children go to their 'home' corners at the beginning of each day where their 'home' teacher plans their day for them. Activity in the work areas is then undertaken by individuals or by groups, and is supervized by the teacher-consultant for that particular field of work. At certain times of each day children return to their 'home' area to report upon the work they have been doing so that a record can be kept. Again, some of our old schools have had the walls between classrooms taken down in order to create conditions for co-operative work. This means that two teachers will have two

* Eveline Lowe Primary School, London, S.E.1.
† Eynsham County Primary School, Nr. Witney, Oxon.

classes together throughout the day and will, of course, keep the children for two years. This organization appears to have certain advantages as the teachers get to know the children very well indeed over this period of time. Parts of the day are given over to one teacher for large-group activities such as music, a story, or a T.V. 'lesson'. Both teachers are available for small-group and individual work; one teacher taking responsibility for work in number (or mathematics), while the other takes responsibility for the language development of all the children and for the detailed recording of this. This cuts down, in some measure, the work of the teacher and the children have two adults in the room to whom they can refer at any time of the day. In some counties, however, twinned classrooms, with a door between them, have been planned for co-operative teaching. In one such case two teachers, with 9 to 11 year old classes, had divided their art and crafts resources so that one was responsible for all the fairly quiet activities such as needlework, painting and collage, whereas the other supervized the noisier activities—woodwork, pottery and model-making. This meant that the children went freely from room to room for materials and help as they worked out their individual and group projects, but at certain times of the day the door could be closed and the children be with their own teacher. This has advantages in schools where children are used to a wide range of activities, in that the teacher does not have to provide, and supervise, every part of this rich environment. In another case, one teacher had a wealth of natural history materials in his classrooms while, next door, the other provided an equally rich environment in poetry and drama. There was no doubt that the children were benefiting from this organization. They flocked from one room to see the badger's brush and to hear the story of finding the sett the previous night and, later in the day, were invited to a session on 'Poems we have Written and Read this Week'.

Some authorities have catered further for this trend by providing a common resource area between two classrooms. Often it is used as a library common to both classes, but sometimes as a quiet place where aural and visual aids, such as the tape-recorder and film loop projector, can be used by small groups. Large and expensive pieces of apparatus can be situated there, and used by the children in both classes. For example, a Language Master* for helping to teach reading could be conveniently located in such an area, especially if the two teachers were either doing some co-operative teaching, or running an integrated day. Besides this additional space for practical work, the throwing open of the two classrooms and the resource area enables the classes to be 'united' at any time. Teachers specializing in their own fields and linked by the resource area, allow their children to move freely. An interesting display of shape, colour or texture by a teacher who is artistically gifted will not only influence the children in the two classes using the resource area, but also will have an effect on the work of the other teacher. Her turn to excite may come when the resource area features 'Science Hidden in Our Playground'. The resource area can also be used as an exhibition space for a project involving both classes. Television lessons are often used as a starting point for this sort of work and, although the broadcast can be looked at and heard by both classes together, the follow-up work may be planned in small groups that cut across the class divisions. For example, following two programmes on the zoo in the ITV series *Seeing and Doing*, one teacher could be responsible for the children's booklets on the background and habits of the animals, while the other could deal with groups of children who wanted, say, to investigate feeding habits or build a model. Sometimes teachers working in this 'twinning' situation will specialize and simply exchange classes. In these instances, although the teachers go from one class to another, the resource area again provides the meeting point and a place where the work can be shown to all groups. Because of this common area one achieves a more integrated and flexible curriculum though some specialization is practised. The resource area can provide, too, a private place to which children can go to prepare a play and put it on tape, before bringing it back into the classroom to be heard by another group.

Many teachers use the corridor space as their resource area,

* Language Master, Bell & Howell machine using taped cards and synchronising printed words or pictures with audio material.

and show their exhibitions for all children to enjoy. Even the cloakroom can sometimes be adapted as a library/exhibition space which forms a common focus for the interests of all the classes. Sometimes it is even used as a place where each teacher takes it in turn, for half-an-hour during the lunch-hour, to read a story to any children who wish to listen. In these co-operative situations children retain all the advantages of belonging to a class but have the advantage, too, of working with other teachers and other groups of children.

One of the main difficulties teachers find as they move from the traditional class pattern to any of these unstructured situations is the problem of keeping records of the work of all the children, not only with regard to their attitudes to learning and their social, emotional and intellectual growth, but also with regard to what the children have actually experienced and learned. Most primary school teachers would need to record the experiences which a child has, the concepts that he forms, the understandings that he acquires, and the skills he is able to use. This, of course, is particularly true of such basic skills as reading, writing, and calculating. There is, too, the recording of the information gathered from reference sources as well as from the ordering of experiences. It is obviously very difficult for a teacher to make detailed records when all the children are doing different things and following their own individual interests and plans of work. However, headteachers of schools where the integrated day is in operation are attempting to list the concepts that children should acquire. In one school the headteacher has listed various mathematics and English concepts, the book in which they can be practised, the materials that the child can use and the apparatus available in the school. The teacher's job is to record each child's progress on a check-list which details the various experiences, concepts, and skills. If the teacher has one age group for more than one year, recording does, however, become a little easier, for, although many things are going on at once, the children, over the long period, become so much more familiar and so much more a part of the group. Of course, in these freer schools many children are able to keep their own records. Often work cards, apparatus, tasks and assignments are designed in such a way that the child can make his own recording. Then, too, in some of the published programmed-reading material, such as that provided by the S.R.A. Labs.,* children keep their own records as part of the system and, once they have learned to do this, it becomes a very easy task for the teacher to know what each child is doing. Children always seem to enjoy filling in their record books and showing their progress by shading graphs with coloured pencils that correspond to the colour of the laboratory suited to their reading level.

In schools changing to an unstructured situation, head-teachers have become increasingly aware of the difficulties of helping new and young staff to deal with the problem of seeing that each child in a class of forty is kept working at various tasks. One headteacher† has written a little booklet, *Making a Start*, for new members of staff. He says: 'Whatever your school may be, the Church, Gothic, Urban Thirties, Post-War with ceiling-to-floor display areas, or new open-plan work areas, you are faced with the need to make the place exciting and stimulating. The school walls should reflect the work of the school, and this means of the teachers and children. A good classroom is a base for all types of work. It is art gallery, museum, workshop, display centre, exhibition area and sales window for education. An alive classroom produces an alive class. You will find children enjoy a home base that is well decorated with your work and theirs. The value of this two-fold approach cannot be over-emphasized. Look round your classroom if in a traditional school, or the work area for which you are responsible if in an open-plan one, and ask yourself "Is it really attractive?", "Will the displays trigger off the children's imagination?", "Are we making the most of the space available?". Remember that display and presentation are so very important to the children in your care, who spend a great deal of time in the school, and try to make the surroundings beautiful, imaginative, stimulating, exciting and enjoyable'. The 'Weather Corner' is suggested as an essential part of any classroom, and he shows how a pictorial method develops through the four

* Scientific Research Associates Reading Laboratories, S.R.A. Ltd., Henley-on-Thames, Oxfordshire.

† Mr Gerald J. Jones, Oldfield C.J. School, Chester, Cheshire.

years at the junior school, from simple recording to quite sophisticated ideas. He makes the point that 'the link with the work in English, maths and art and crafts is tremendous', and that 'simple weather instruments can also be made as part of the science scheme'. His illustrative panel is shown below.

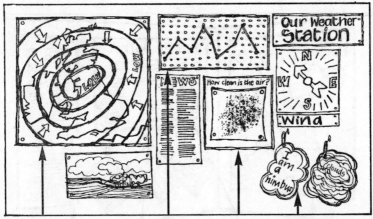

A map showing weather areas covered with clear plastic sheeting which allows information to be written on it with a chinagraph pencil and then wiped off.

Peg-boarding makes an ideal graph board to show temperature.

Soak a piece of lint in water and then place on a roof area for a week; this will clearly show carbon deposit.

Make books to illustrate weather to be associated with cloud types

Other possible book titles are 'Our Weather Records', 'Our Collection of Weather Sayings', and 'I am a Cumulus Cloud'. Another suggestion is that one part of the classroom be devoted to what may be termed 'English'. The illustration on p. 148 shows the 'Book of the Month' and an item called 'Meet the Authors', together with a further illustration of a poem.

Booklets on such topics as 'My Favourite TV Programme', 'I should like to be . . .', 'My Favourite Recipe' and 'The Book I Enjoyed Most', give the children outlets for work when other topics are finished. They are also useful to take home for extra work. Another useful resource is 'the dressing-up box'. Oddments for this can be collected well before term begins.

Interesting material—hats, belts, old curios, etc.—will be invaluable when doing informal drama.

The benefits of having areas and corners devoted to mathematics and science have been mentioned in earlier chapters. The science corner may well include an assortment of natural materials which the children have brought to school,

'Book of the Month'. It is a good idea to choose one book for reading aloud to your children during your 'teacher's time'. This may produce interesting art work in the form shown, which is a picture done by a group of children as part of a class book.

'Meet the Author'. Children like to know about writers.

Group and individual booklets should be the order of the day.

A poem, well written and illustrated, is useful as an appetite promoter.

or even a miniature zoo with hamsters, rabbits, mice, fish, stick-insects and so on. An indoor garden containing house plants, bulbs and mosses ensures that the nature area is alive all the year round.

Other suggestions for display corners come quickly to mind: after the summer holiday, a collection of shells; after an exhibition of carvings brought in by the teacher, a collection of pieces of wood of all shapes and sizes. A history project could lead to a display of models. Child-size figures can be constructed in cardboard and painted, brass-rubbings can be made, and maps and souvenirs collected. These will help to create an exciting history corner.

As the classroom now seems to contain more than four corners, it is obvious that the furniture must be arranged to form small areas and working booths.

The diagram shows how four pieces of corrugated cardboard of varying heights can give a room a new pattern where work areas, library areas and other activity spaces can be developed without difficulty. Extra display space is available and children's work can be fixed to the board using sellotape, staples or map pins. It is, of course, possible to move cupboards,

Conventional classroom pattern   Pattern changed — bird's-eye view

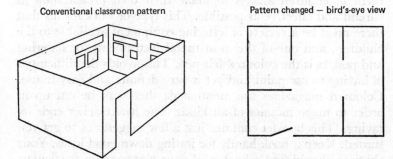

bookcases and even the piano out at right-angles to the wall as a means of making extra working bays. Having provided all this extra display space, the teacher now needs much more paper than is usually available from stock and will have to seek out other sources such as the local wallpaper stores which often sell cheap rolls of lining paper, the local decorator who will often have odd lengths to give away, or even the local newspaper printers, who, because of machine limitations, have a wastage on each roll of newsprint which can be got either very cheaply or free of charge. Other teachers have found a new material and another source—many factories which pack or unpack materials, especially scientific instruments, throw away the expanded polystyrene packing. This is an extremely easy material to use, soft enough to carve, easy to paint and rigid enough for model-making. Recently I saw 9″ × 9″ squares of this material carved and painted by individual children, and put one above the other on the wall to make the most glorious totem pole. In most classrooms today one sees poly-styrene being used for modelling and for creative work, as it sometimes comes in pieces that are quite thick enough to allow for a considerable amount of interesting sculpture. Of course, no little pamphlet called 'Making a Start' would be complete without a 'Ways and Means' section, and there are suggestions for using the ceiling for any diagrams of the constellations, or for the compass points, or even for the positions of the surrounding towns. It deals, too, with such questions as presentation, the different coloured papers on which children's own paintings are mounted, and the encourage-ment of children always to make their own presentation as careful and effective as possible. This type of work means that there must be a variety of lettering equipment available to the children, and one of the most useful instruments for lettering and posters is the coloured felt pen. This avoids the difficulties of having to use paint and yet is very definite and easy to use. Coloured magazines are mentioned; these can be cut up in order to make mosaics of all kinds. The headteacher ends by saying, 'This booklet contains just a few suggestions to get you started. Keep a book handy for jotting down good ideas. Your children should find school, and your classroom in particular, a place of excitement, enjoyment and employment.'

One of the most interesting results of these developments is that the rôle of the headteacher is changing rapidly. In the flexible school he is seldom in the Head's room but in and out of the classrooms helping groups and individual children. In fact, in the new schools the Head no longer has a room furnished like an office but probably has instead a small, comfortable place with a coffee table where he can talk to parents in an informal way, while the secretary probably has an even smaller office next door. If the school is running on experimental lines, the Head will probably need to spend much more time with the children, and in explaining the aims of the experiment to their parents who will want to know what is happening. The headmaster of one new junior school,* where 7+ to 11+ children are grouped in each class, sends

* Mr C. Betty, Lordswood C.J. School, Chatham, Kent.

out a booklet to explain his policy of Vertical Grouping, and to invite parents to take part in the work of the school. This booklet is in the form of an eighteen-page half-quarto letter in which the Head explains in simple terms what he is trying to do. It deals with the curriculum and the fact that children are helped to learn by 'discovery'. It shows how the library is used and asks for parental help in all sorts of activities in and out of the schoool. It describes the work of the two evening clubs where parents and children attend together, the work of the Adult Education Centre and the Parent-Teacher Association. It deals, too, with a new type of report, in the form of a letter, that he intends to give to each parent. This new function means that the headteacher must really work with, and know, every child inside the classroom and not meet him only when he comes to show his 'best' or his 'worst' work.

At another school where team teaching was being tried for the first time, the headteacher* acted as the team leader, as the diagram on p. 152 makes clear.

Team Teaching Topic: 'Our City' (approximately 70 children, two classes of 10 to 11 year olds).
Time Allocation: 1½ days per week for ten weeks (approximately seven 'Key lessons', two films, seven visits for each group; the rest of the time was spent in work periods, group reporting and work for an exhibition).
Teaching Team: Headteacher.
               Two assistant teachers.
Group Leaders: Eight student teachers.

Not only was he involved in giving some of the 'key' lessons to the full group of children, but also he took part in the work periods that followed each of the seven visits made by the small groups, helping the student teachers who were responsible for these, as well as working out a quite complicated timetable of visits and work periods for the ten-week experiment. This rôle of team leader with all its implications of co-operative planning and the free discussion with groups of children, student teachers and teachers in the work periods, gives the Head a different kind of contact with both staff and children,

* Mr Gerald J. Jones, Oldfield C.J. Junior School, Chester, Cheshire.
C.A.S.—11

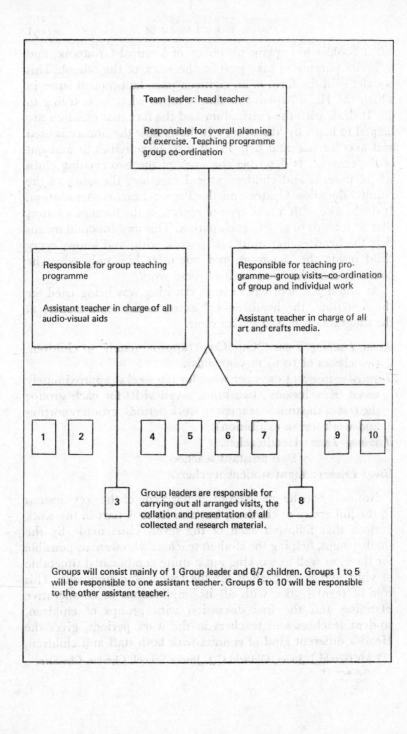

Team leader: head teacher

Responsible for overall planning of exercise. Teaching programme group co-ordination

Responsible for group teaching programme

Assistant teacher in charge of all audio-visual aids

Responsible for teaching programme—group visits—co-ordination of group and individual work

Assistant teacher in charge of all art and crafts media.

1 2 4 5 6 7 9 10

3 Group leaders are responsible for carrying out all arranged visits, the collation and presentation of all collected and research material. 8

Groups will consist mainly of 1 Group leader and 6/7 children. Groups 1 to 5 will be responsible to one assistant teacher. Groups 6 to 10 will be responsible to the other assistant teacher.

and takes him, as well as the teachers and children, out of the classroom 'box' situation.

The teachers in our primary schools are genuinely concerned that they can no longer deal with everything that all the children in one class need, and many experiments are going on in order to find ways of making it easier to do this. In one such, children learn about their environment through a Programmed Learning Multi-Media Approach.* Thirty different programmed booklets on, for example, roads, railways, canals, transport and farming, are being written in such a way that pairs of children can work on these, more or less, without help. Kits of material provide the audio-visual aids that are needed, visits are indicated in the programmes, parental help is being used and children seem to be very happy to work in this way. They can, in fact, work from 9 a.m. to 4 p.m. without losing interest. Of course, the reading of the programme presents some problems to slow learners, but this has been overcome by providing an audio-visual dictionary on a Language Master so that children can listen to a word they do not know as well as look at it, and then hear its meaning. The interests of junior children have been built into the programme and they are asked to collect certain material, to interview people, to look at slides, to make a tape, to write a play, to build a model and so on. Their traditional classroom becomes, for the day, a series of small home-made booths in which children work together on different programmes, display their paintings, written work and models, or move about the room freely in order to do what is indicated in their particular programmed booklet. One advantage of this type of approach is that teachers are helped by having worked out for them, in the programmes, the usual data about the environment that children might be expected to learn in the primary school. The method is self-instructional in that the programmes can be used by the children to check the accuracy of their discoveries with very little help from the teacher. It is interesting enough for the children not to become bored, to work independently, and to acquire many social skills

* A Nuffield Resources for Learning Project experiment at Binley Junior School, Coventry—Headmaster, Mr D. Young; programmes, Mr Colin Kefford; publisher, Blandford Press.

as they progress through the tasks required by the programmes. To go into this classroom when this approach is in use is to find children, in pairs, looking at a film-loop on a canal lock, reading the programmed booklet in order to find out how to classify traffic when they do their census, or about to visit a local farm with questionnaires in hand and a parent in charge.

Parents and student teachers are increasingly being used to meet the demands of modern trends but they are not the only extra adults you might find in the primary classroom today. One current experiment is concerned with the enrichment of one or two schools in depressed areas. One particular school has been equipped with a full service of television, video-tape recorder and radio, while another has been supplied with as many audio-visual aids as possible, in addition to television and radio. In both cases a technical assistant has been appointed for two years in order to see whether the primary school classroom will gain anything from this type of appointment. He will not only service the equipment and help the teachers and children to use it, but will also, it is hoped, become a 'Resources Officer' in that teachers will rely on him to make and produce supplementary material as they need it. Some stimulating experience on television or radio may result in a long-term project and involve him in the preparation of slides or teaching loops; it may even lead to the making of kits of material so that groups of children can 'find out for themselves'.

The more active the classroom becomes, the more usefully can adults be engaged in helping the children, and the more self-instructional material will be required. Teachers are now putting their reading schemes, stories, children's own poems and plays on tape and one will often see half-a-dozen children grouped round a tape recorder with their six little sets of plastic headphones following a 'reading lesson' from their books. One of our real difficulties, especially with deprived children, is to get enough communication between groups and individuals in the classroom, and the advantages of having extra adult help and using more audio-visual material are obvious. Publishers are, of course, aware of this and, in addition to material made by the teacher, kits such as the Avipak series for teaching creative writing are being produced. This set includes teaching notes, a tape with four, open-ended stories and a musical section for use with transparencies, four sets of picture cards showing sequences in open-ended adventure situations, and four slide sets entitled 'The Mediaeval Manor', 'Logging', 'A Knight and his Training' and 'Mars'. It claims to be the material for twelve half-hour English lessons. Kits such as these are certainly being used and are helpful in some teaching situations, but most progressive schools integrate English with all other work and would not accept that the kits could lead to the individual experiences that inspire the best creative writing.

The teaching machine, too, is to be found in the primary classroom and, in a current experiment, some self-instructional reading aids are being tried out. These are the Language Master, the Talking Page* and various other devices that include the use of picture, word and voice for teaching reading. The Language Master allows teachers to produce their own reading programmes which the children can put into the machine and play through. Children used to this device seem to like it and are able to work by themselves for a considerable length of time as long as the teacher-tape indicates interesting activities usually concerned with drawing, writing and speaking. The Talking Page uses programmes on plastic discs designed to teach English to immigrants, reading to 5 year olds and modern mathematics. There are plans, too, for programmes on music and French. This particular device is interesting in that the pictures, the written word and the spoken word are synchronized. Also, the child has a choice of buttons to press when he gives the answer and the machine then corrects him. He is also able to return to any point in the 'conversation'. This use of aids is probably one of the really important developments in the primary classroom, especially as they can be used in an individual situation, with headphones, for independent study. These developments are a long way off for many of us, as the equipment is extremely expensive, and are certainly quite remote for those countries which have less money to spend on primary education than we. However, as the primary years are so important in building the attitudes towards any job that

* Rank-R.E.C. Limited, 11 Belgrave Road, London, S.W.1.

requires initiative, independent thought and imagination, it may be as well to explore the possibilities of technology very fully as far as this age group is concerned, even to the point of providing a closed circuit television unit in each school so that primary and other teachers can share their specialist skills without losing what is one of the most important things in our primary schools, the close contact between child and teacher.

FOR FURTHER READING

Sealey, L. G. W., and Gibbon, Vivian, *Communication and Learning in the Primary School*, Blackwell, 1962.

Using Books in the Primary School, School Library Association.

Sturt, Felicity, (an annotated list), *Primary School Library Books*, School Library Association, 1968.

Blackie, John, *Inside the Primary School*, H.M.S.O., 1967.

Razzell, Arthur, *Juniors*, Penguin Special, 1968.

12. Spreading the New Ideas

G. B. Corston

IN THE previous chapters we have read of the vast changes that have taken place in the curriculum of the British primary school during the last decade, and the effect these changes have had on classroom practice. In many of the subjects mentioned in this book, there has been a change in the content presented to the children, for instance, the subject matter of primary mathematics has been revised considerably and in many schools an entirely new subject, French, has been introduced. These changes in content, however, have been accompanied by changes in the way subjects are taught, or, rather changes in the way in which children are encouraged to learn. These two aspects cannot be treated separately, for much of the new subject content has brought about a change in teaching methods; in many cases it has forced teachers to review and revise their teaching techniques as, for example, in the case of science. Of course, there were other factors which affected teaching methods, notably the views on the way in which children learn which result from the work of developmental psychologists. But, returning to my previous point, we see that content and method very often go together; a change in one can bring about a change in the other, or both may change together. In primary schools the emphasis appears to have been more on a change of method with a subsequent, and natural, change in content.

Obviously if we are concerned with changes in the classroom, changes introduced for the benefit of children—and let us not forget that schools are built for children—this will also mean a change for the majority of teachers. In the past most of the innovations, the progressive changes in primary education, came from the training colleges—these were the leaders. However, many of the current developments such as those described in this book originated from other sources, from inspectors and advisers, both national and local, and above all from talented and imaginative teachers actively engaged in the day-to-day business of working with children. There were of course, some leads from equally far-seeing people engaged in teacher training, but, for a brief spell, many of the colleges lagged behind, and found themselves having to follow the lead coming from the schools and other sources mentioned.

For the vast majority of trained and experienced teachers these changes have meant a serious re-thinking of ideas and some re-training. The development of the curriculum is closely bound up with changes in the methods and attitudes of teachers. These should be moulded in their initial training, but opportunities must be provided for continual professional re-education throughout a teacher's career. We shall now look at how this was tackled and how the business of spreading the new ideas was, and is being, brought about.

Perhaps the most significant factor in the re-education of teachers already serving in schools—in-service training as it is sometimes called as distinct from pre-service or initial training in colleges—has been the setting up of Teachers' Centres. Many of the new ideas which had developed in small pockets in various parts of the country have been brought together and planned in a more structured way on a wider basis by such bodies as the Schools Council, the Nuffield Foundation and the Scottish Education Department. With their greater resources these bodies have been able to draw together the best ideas being tried out, to plan a progressive development and to present them to a wider audience. This has been the practice, for instance, in the teaching of French, mathematics and science. It had often been found that the teachers' enthusiasm and interest for the new ideas, which had been aroused by short courses of a few days' duration, gradually declined unless there was fairly intensive and sustained follow-up. In a few places this was achieved by regular meetings or study groups set up by teachers themselves, and in others by the advice and guidance given by such people as local authority advisers and inspectors. In places where this did not happen, the majority of teachers soon reverted to their former practices in the classroom. This study-group type of follow-up gave a hint to ways in which future in-service training could be organized and as a result, at the time of their initiation, the Nuffield Mathematics Teaching Project and the Nuffield Junior Science Project insisted that participating local education authorities should establish Teachers' Centres. Of these the Schools Council publication *Curriculum Development: Teachers' Groups and Centres* says 'the essence of curriculum review and development is new thinking by teachers themselves, as well as their appraisal of the thinking of others. Teachers should have regular opportunities to meet together. They should look upon the initiation of thought, as well as the trial and assessment of new ideas and procedure, as an integral part of their professional service to society'.

The same paper suggests three possible ways in which a local Centre can operate:

(a) to focus local interest and to give teachers a setting within which new objectives can be discussed and defined and new ideas aired;

(b) the schools in the area of a local group may be among those which have been formally invited to give new materials their trial before publication (e.g. in the Nuffield Mathematics Teaching Project) in which case the local centre will contribute to the evaluation of materials and feed back comments, criticisms and suggestions for improvement;

(c) where teachers are not involved in the trial of work being developed nationally they should be kept informed about research and development in progress elsewhere.

Such is the organization of education in this country, where each local authority is left to decide for itself what it wants and needs, that no two Teachers' Centres are alike. Many began as Centres directly associated with the development of a national project, others as much broader-based Curriculum Development Centres. But although there is this wide variety there are common aims. Essentially the Centres are places where teachers can meet informally to discuss ideas among themselves, and where in-service courses for teachers can be held. Despite the work of the subject associations, many teachers, in the past, kept very much to their own schools and knew little of what went on elsewhere. Now at the Centres we see teachers from different schools and from different stages of education talking and thinking together. New methods of teaching, new schemes of work, new ideas can be proposed, but they will lead nowhere without a lively attitude on the part of the teachers. It is the function of the Teachers' Centre to inform teachers of these developments, to generate enthusiasm and to encourage them to follow these leads.

Let us first look at the way in which a large-scale project works, and then go on to see how other local development takes place. Usually when such a project is launched, a small team is appointed to produce materials and suggest ideas as starting points, and various areas in the country are invited to take part in testing the materials. A course is normally held to bring together area organizers, the people who will largely be responsible for seeing that Centres are set up and facilities made available for spreading the ideas in their areas. Such courses, of say a week's duration, are usually staffed by members of Her Majesty's Inspectorate and the project team, who outline the aims of the project's work as it is to be developed in the schools. The area organizers then go back to their different localities and start meetings at their Centres. The next stage is for similar courses to be held for teacher-leaders. These are the people who will be involved in leading the work at the Centre—in some cases they will be local advisers and inspectors, but more often they are teachers who have been selected, because of their interest and enthusiasm, to lead the courses and discussions for their colleagues. By this time the Centres are already being used for courses and meetings for serving teachers connected with the project, and work is being started in the schools. So we see the third stage in the spread of ideas; teachers representing the schools engaged in the project activities meeting locally under the leadership of colleagues who have been on national courses. These teachers further spread the ideas among other colleagues in their own schools. Later on, as more areas in the country want to take part, the plan outlined above is repeated. The enthusiasm generated at the Teachers' Centre infects other teachers in the area, more schools wish to become involved in the work and more teachers join in the courses and meetings at the Centre. In this way we have both a planned, structured approach to the development of the project—from national courses, through the local Centres to the schools—and a more informal spread of ideas through interest aroused in a particular area being caught by other teachers and then concentrated at the Teachers' Centre. Sooner or later the direct influence of the project team diminishes but the activities established in schools carry on and the Centre is the key point for continued local development. It is clear that once a Centre has been established and work started in the schools any continued, progressive development depends on effective local leadership. No longer do we meet the situation which existed up to five years ago where individual teachers attended courses, both short and long term, on subjects in which they were interested and then returned occasionally to try out their newly-gained knowledge in their own classes and to keep it to themselves—or more often than not, not even to try out the ideas but to lock them away in the cupboards of the mind. Now the Centre provides the hub from which ideas radiate to the schools. It too, however, would soon cease to be effective without local leadership, which, to be a success, must come from among serving teachers. In some places the local administration selects teacher-leaders, in others they are naturally selected by their colleagues. However they are chosen, it is important that they have not only experience and skill, but are acceptable to, and respected by, their colleagues. Even with expert leadership and with teachers sharing responsibility for some of their own professional training, some overall authority is needed on the administrative side to keep the Centre working at maximum efficiency. It is notable that perhaps the most successful Teachers' Centres are those where the local inspectors or advisers accept responsibility for curriculum development and in-service training as part of their work, where a warden, full-time or part-time, is in charge of the day-to-day running of the Centre (if part-time, he works part-time in schools assisting with the development of new work) and where, under this leadership and direction, teachers take a full part in spreading the new ideas either through a small organizing committee, or by supplying their own teacher-leaders for courses or, better still, by both.

Earlier in this chapter it was said that, for a time, the Colleges of Education responsible for the initial training of teachers appeared to lag behind in the spreading of new ideas. This is no longer so and the colleges play their full part in the development of the primary school curriculum. For, in addition to their specific task of initial training, they also help with in-service training. After all, teacher training should be considered as a continuous process, not stopping at the end of college. For years we have paid lip-service to the principle that initial college training should be the first part of teacher training, to be followed by the first period of service in schools as further training. Now with teachers playing a larger part in their own professional training through subject associations and involvement in local and national curriculum development projects, it is becoming a reality. The spread of ideas to established teachers through in-service training should follow naturally upon the start made in the initial training period, which can only be a preparation for teaching. There is great value, then, in drawing upon the college lecturers' knowledge of both subject matter and training methods. This is a two-way traffic. The use of lecturers working with teachers at the Centre is of benefit to both. The teachers have the expert knowledge, advice and assistance from the lecturers. The colleges gain by a closer association with the schools, they know more of the actual curriculum development taking place in the classroom and can prepare their students more satisfactorily for teaching practice and first appointments. Some of the closest co-operation has occurred where a Teachers' Centre has been set up in an existing College of Education. One obvious advantage of this is that the facilities which already exist in the college can be made available to teachers.

Of course, the spreading of new ideas is not limited to the activities emanating from a Teachers' Centre. As we have earlier remarked, subject associations, such as the Association of Teachers of Mathematics, have played a great part in developing and spreading new ideas. In addition, for many years, courses varying in length from a few days to many weeks, have been organized by the Department of Education and Science, by local authorities, and by Institutes of Education. Many of these can be looked upon as refresher courses to 'refresh' teachers' minds and to set them thinking and talking about some of the new ideas. They can do little more than this because of the short length of the majority of the courses, but at least they are starting points, and as mentioned earlier, they become of significant value when there are facilities for following up these ideas at working level in the schools. This again is where the Centres play their part.

We have already seen how Colleges of Education have again assumed their rightful place in promoting the spread of new ideas for their students on initial training courses, have begun to assist with in-service training courses at Centres, and in some cases, have Centres in their buildings. There is another way in which they have a marked effect on spreading new ideas and this is through the courses for experienced teachers which many colleges now organize. These courses are normally of one term's duration, specialize in one subject, and are intended for teachers who have been teaching for some years and who are keen to introduce new work into their schools but who did not meet the new ideas and content during their initial training. On a course of this length, much more time can be spent in really seeing how new ideas, already discussed in theory, can actually be put into practice. The number of teachers on any one such course is usually about fifteen to twenty. This enables the courses to be run as 'workshops', with the teachers actively engaged in their own learning rather than sitting and listening to lecturers. They have to *do* something positive themselves. The courses enjoy all the college facilities and are run by college lecturers. To see how new ideas are put into practice, part of the time is spent on school visits, where the course members have the opportunity of seeing progressive teachers at work. These are of enormous value, for teachers will always ask how they are to introduce new ideas with a class of forty children, and will accept suggestions from colleagues engaged in day-to-day teaching more readily than from a course lecturer talking in general terms.

These supplementary courses, as they are called, are one

way of producing informed teacher-leaders who can go back to their own districts and take a leading part in curriculum development there, and are also an excellent way of giving experienced teachers a good, hard look at new ideas. Experienced teachers often find the greatest difficulty in changing both their thoughts about children's learning and their own teaching techniques, and therefore benefit most from this help and advice. Unfortunately in some areas it has not been easy to release a teacher for as long as a term and find a replacement for his class—paradoxically it is sometimes more convenient to give leave of absence for a whole school year. Nevertheless, these one-term courses have a useful part to play in the overall organization of in-service training of teachers, particularly in providing future leaders for curriculum development from within the teaching profession itself. Even at the risk of appearing to over-emphasize this point of using teachers to assist colleagues in their professional training, it is worth stating again that teachers do in fact seem keen to take the lead from their more progressive and informed colleagues, and this has been the most influential means of spreading ideas. This is also seen in another way. Not only are teacher-leaders playing an important part in furthering development, but, once teachers wish to introduce new work into their own schools, they should be able to visit colleagues in schools already committed, to see work actually going on with children—that is, the ideas being put into practice. This has certainly happened in the case of primary mathematics and science, two of the subjects in which many highly competent teachers have felt the need for practical help in the classroom as well as with their own personal understanding of the subject. Teachers gain reassurance and confidence to tackle new methods from inter-school visits. As a further extension to this, in some areas a group of teachers has held meetings in rotation in each other's schools. On a wider scale, again after an initial start has been made, the spread of ideas is accelerated through an interchange at regional level where teacher-leaders and advisers involved in the work at a Teachers' Centre will visit colleagues doing similar work in another area. Not only does this help the spread of new ideas, but teachers will realize that, wherever they work, there are common problems and will be encouraged to come together to discuss the different ways in which these can be tackled.

One other way of spreading ideas is employed by the large-scale projects organized on a national basis. While every encouragement is given to teachers to develop their own ideas, more directed guidance is usually provided in Teachers' Guides. Very few, if any, of these projects provide pupils' materials, but instead produce Guides for teachers. Generally these explain the philosophy of the project, the principles involved in its teaching methods, and give some indication of how to introduce appropriate activities in the classroom. In nearly every case it is emphasized that the teachers are free to teach in any way they wish, and that there is no one set way of introducing and developing the ideas outlined in the project. In short, the Guides are no more than guides. In no sense is the teacher given a detailed programme to be followed, nor do the Guides lay down a syllabus. They do, however, form a very real part of the whole business of spreading ideas, and frequently are the basis for discussion at Teachers' Centres. Before introducing activities from these Guides to the classroom, teachers will examine them carefully and critically with each other—and will continue this appraisal throughout the time the Guides are being used.

In some spheres of primary curriculum activity there has been an additional aid in providing teachers with information and material for discussion, namely television. For many years now, both television and radio have been used for school programmes, that is actual broadcast lessons for pupils, and more recently television programmes for adult education have been produced, including some to inform parents of current developments in educational practice. It is only during the last two years that television programmes specifically for teachers have been broadcast. Two notable series were on primary mathematics and primary science. These programmes showed children and teachers engaged in activities associated with the Nuffield projects, and also teachers working at Teachers' Centres. As television can reach a very wide audience, these series were particularly useful in spreading the news to places where teachers were on the verge of making a start but where there was little chance of contact with more experienced teachers, and also in furnishing material for discussion in Centres already established.

So far we have looked in a very general way at the methods by which new ideas in primary school activities are being spread, with the Teachers' Centres now springing up in large numbers in this country literally being at the centre—the receiving centre into which wide-scale project ideas are fed, and then from which they radiate to the local schools. But all this has been very general. It has already been pointed out that each local authority is free to develop its Centre, or Centres, in whatever way it thinks is likely to be the most effective, and so no two Centres are exactly alike. Yet there are common factors. To conclude this chapter then, we show how curriculum development and the Teachers' Centre are organized in one particular area. In many ways one would hope that this is typical of many such arrangements, but it must be emphasized that what follows is not intended as an example of the ideal situation.

The Teachers' Centre in this authority occupies the top floor of a three-storey Victorian school building. The floor is no longer required by pupils, as the infants' school is on the ground floor, the juniors' on the next, and the senior (secondary) pupils who formerly occupied the top floor are housed in new buildings.

The authority was selected as a pilot area for the Nuffield Mathematics Project, and the pilot schools began work in September 1965. In December 1964 three rooms were available and these were used as a Mathematics Centre for the teachers directly involved in the project. The courses began, then, some nine months before the materials were available in the schools. From September 1965 two members of the original Nuffield development team who had been appointed to the authority's Inspectorate were responsible for weekly in-service courses for teachers. Early in 1966 an experienced primary school teacher with an enthusiasm for modern methods in mathematics teaching was appointed to co-ordinate the work in the schools engaged in Nuffield Mathematics, and to assist in the administration of the Teachers' Centre and the conduct of in-service training in mathematics there. When the administrative duties involved in the day-to-day running of the Mathematics Centre increased, he was given part-time secretarial assistance. From then, the Centre's facilities have expanded so rapidly and extensively that no longer are its activities confined to mathematics. It can now be called a Teachers' Centre, or even a Curriculum Development Centre. A Leader of Curriculum Studies, mainly at secondary level, has been appointed and the secretarial assistance increased to almost full-time. In addition to the mathematics practical rooms there is a library which is attractively furnished and equipped with books of reference and magazines for the exclusive use of teachers, a comfortable conference room, a teachers' workshop with gas and electrical power points and formica-topped benches equipped with wood- and metal-working tools, an audio-visual lecture room and a secondary curriculum room. There are also two smaller rooms, one used as an office and the other for interviews and small group discussions. A model infants' classroom, the exhibits in which will be frequently changed, is being set up in the last of the former classrooms on this floor. All these rooms are grouped round a central hall which can be used for large meetings or for exhibitions and displays of children's or other work. Adult cloakrooms and lavatories have been provided and also a coffee and tea bar. The initial cost of modifying the existing facilities was about £2,000. This covered decorating, the minor alterations needed to provide adequate heating and the building of extra toilet accommodation. A further sum of about £800 was spent on furniture and equipment to start the Mathematics Centre working. Each year the continued development of the Centre has meant extra expenditure of about £300 per annum for apparatus and equipment, and £300/£400 for furniture.

The range of activities has increased at a correspondingly rapid rate. From the early mathematics courses intended for the teachers from the eight Nuffield pilot schools, and which took place on one afternoon each week, courses for teachers now cover a wide range of curricular activities and arise from different sources. These include:

(a) courses run by the authority's Inspectors for untrained entrants to the profession,

(b) in-service training courses run by the Inspectors to present the latest thinking about subject teaching,

(c) courses which run continuously as part of national development projects, for example, in mathematics and science,

(d) courses organized by outside bodies, such as the University of London Institute of Education,

(e) occasional courses of the Department of Education and Science.

So extensive was the range of activities developed in the Centre that the accommodation became seriously strained and difficulty arose in catering for so many interests in one place. To ease the pressure on the working areas, courses in Art and Drama were moved to a second Centre set up on the ground floor of an old school. This Art/Drama Centre provided sufficient space for courses on movement and educational drama, and rooms which could be set aside specifically for 'messy' crafts. In addition to definite in-service courses in Art and Drama to assist classroom practice, there has been a further interesting development. Two Children's Theatre Groups composed of teachers in the authority have been formed and these provide activities, rather than performances, for children after school in some of the primary schools. Not only is this of great value in enabling children to participate in their own drama under expert guidance, but it serves as an example for the ordinary class teachers who can build on the start made, and indirectly receive some re-education themselves.

Approximately 60 per cent of all the teachers employed by the authority use the Centre at least once a term. For example, in the Autumn Term of 1967, out of a teaching force of about 1,500, some 820 made 3,000 attendances altogether. To involve the teachers even more closely in their own professional re-education and to make full use of the developing facilities at the Centre, there is now a scheme whereby, once a year, teachers are given the opportunity to indicate particular fields of the curriculum in which they would like courses arranged during the following academic year. Voluntary and professional associations of teachers also make use of the Centre for meetings. For example, the local Teachers' Careers Guidance and Audio-Visual Aids Associations and the history, geography and mathematics subject associations use the facilities for meetings and conferences.

The Teachers' Centre also provides the logical place for regular meetings, both formal and informal, of teachers from the whole range of the school organization—secondary and primary. There is a temptation for teachers to blame their colleagues in the preceding section of the school system for deficiencies in their pupils' learning. One of the most successful and gratifying features of the establishment of the Teachers' Centre has been the breaking down of the previous rigid structure. Now colleagues from all strata come together to discuss common problems. Not only is the Centre used for spreading information through courses, books and magazines, but the teacher-in-charge publishes once a term a 'Newsletter' which goes to all schools in the Borough and to Teachers' Centres in other authorities. The early issues were confined to news and information about primary mathematics written entirely by the teacher-in-charge. Now there is a small committee which acts as an editorial body and the information covers a much wider field, including news about new publications, equipment and sources of supply. The Secondary Curriculum Development Leader also issues a bulletin once a term called 'Project', mainly concerned with giving information about resources available for secondary activities.

So much for the development of this Teachers' Centre. Most of the discussion has been about its part in primary school curriculum affairs, but an almost equally lengthy account could have been written on secondary school matters. To conclude, we look at a specific example of how one piece of curriculum development, that in primary mathematics, has spread through the influence of the Teachers' Centre.

In the authority there are eighty-eight primary schools. Of these, in September 1965, eight schools (four infant and four junior) started activities as pilot schools in the Nuffield Project. These schools had been invited to take part in this work in December 1964 and from that time teachers from the schools had attended courses at the Centre on one afternoon each week. This continued in 1965/66 when the Nuffield materials were being used. The interest these, and other courses in mathematics, aroused led to a further fourteen schools joining in September 1966 and, with the appointment of the teacher-in-charge at the Centre, courses were then held on two afternoons each week. These were organized in two sections—one set for beginners, that is teachers wishing to embark on a more progressive approach to mathematics teaching, and the other for the teachers already working on these lines who needed ideas for further development and also opportunities to improve their own knowledge of mathematics. With the general publication of the Nuffield Teachers' Guides in September 1967 yet more schools became involved, so now almost half the primary schools in the authority are represented on courses at various times, covering a wide range of involvement from those just mildly interested to those fully committed.

The establishment of Teachers' Centres, in which groups of teachers can be associated with their own development work, is as important an innovation as some of the more frequently discussed ones concerning school re-organization. Educational experiments of real value cannot be imposed from sources outside the schools. They must be worked out, and worked upon, by those who are going to be responsible for their development, the teachers in the schools. Teachers actively involved in experiment and development become better teachers.

Establishing a Teachers' Centre on the lines outlined in this chapter is probably the least expensive and most effective way for an authority to achieve this end.

FOR FURTHER READING

Schools Council Working Paper No. 10, *Curriculum Development. Teachers' Groups and Centres*, H.M.S.O., 1967.

NOTES ON THE CONTRIBUTORS

JOHN ALLEN. H.M. Inspector with national responsibility for drama; scriptwriter and producer, School Broadcasting Department of B.B.C.; administrator and producer, Glyndebourne Children's Theatre.

JACK BACKHOUSE. Headmaster, Oyster Park Junior School, Castleford, and formerly a teacher in secondary and primary schools.

JOHN BLACKIE, C.B. H.M. Inspector of Schools 1933–66; Chief Inspector of Primary Schools 1958–66; part-time lecturer, Homerton College of Education, Cambridge.

FRANK BLACKWELL. Inspector for Croydon Borough; formerly headmaster of a Ramsgate school and a member of the Nuffield Junior Science Project team.

ENA CORMACK. Assistant Adviser in Primary Education in Edinburgh; formerly a primary school teacher.

GEORGE CORSTON. General Inspector of Primary Schools, London Borough of Newham; formerly a member of the Nuffield Foundation Mathematics Teaching Project, and a headmaster of primary schools.

JUNE DERRICK. Organiser of the Schools Council Project in English for Immigrant Children; formerly Lecturer in Contemporary English at the University of Leeds and a teacher of English in the U.K. and overseas.

RUTH FOSTER. Vice-Principal of Dartington College of Arts, and Head of the Dance and Drama Department; formerly H.M. Inspector of Schools.

DAVID MACKAY. A member of the Schools Council Programme in Linguistics and English Teaching at University College London; formerly headmaster of a primary school in a depressed area in London.

171

SYBIL MARSHALL. Reader in Primary Education at the University of Sussex and the author of several books on education; formerly a class teacher and headteacher.

DAVID ROWLANDS. Deputy Director of the Schools Council Modern Languages Project and organiser of the Spanish section; formerly a member of the team which produced the Nuffield course *En Avant*, and a language teacher in Northern Ireland.

Mrs E. BAY TIDY, O.B.E. Primary adviser to the Nuffield Foundation Resources for Learning Project; formerly headmistress of primary and secondary schools and Head of the Education Department at Coventry College of Education.